M000081457

Table of Contents

Foreword 9

Introduction 13

Chapter 1: Commit and Take Daily Action 21

Chapter 2: Launch a Healthy Life.................................33

Chapter 3: Your No-Cost On-Call Therapist 43

Chapter 4: Discover Your Power.................................53

Chapter 5: Express Your Emotions.............................61

Chapter 6: Rekindle the Light in Your Life 73

Chapter 7: Create a New Life Story............................83

Chapter 8: Design Your Future 93

Chapter 9: Manifest a Life You Love 103

Chapter 10: Manage Your Mind 113

Chapter 11: Nurture Your Inner Wisdom 124

Chapter 12: Love Yourself More!...............................133

Acknowledgements...137

About the Author...139

Heal Yourself
with Journaling Power

Mari L. McCarthy

Copyright © 2019 Mari L. McCarthy

All rights reserved. No part of this book may be reproduced, distributed or transmitted in any form, or by any means, or stored in a database or retrieval systems without prior expressed written permission of the author of this book.

ISBN: 978-1-5356-1677-5

Praise for *Heal Yourself with Journaling Power*

"In a world of everpresent scary news, stress, and technology that distracts us from genuine human encounters, Mari McCarthy invites us to do something both simple and radical: Pause daily to encounter our own souls. And she not only tells us to *just do it*, she shows us how with her own life story, the stories of others, and her many ideas about how to maximize the transformative power of journaling time."

Kevin Anderson, Ph.D., Author of *Now is Where God Lives: A Year of Nested Meditations to Delight the Mind and Awaken the Soul* and *The Inconceivable Surprise of Living: Sustaining Wisdom for Spiritual Beings Trying to Be Human.*

"The most important lesson illustrated in Heal Yourself with Journaling Power is that anyone can enhance their health and wellbeing through the therapeutic power of expressive writing. This is the definitive book that shows you how. So just grab a pen and a pad of paper and do it!"

Mike Bundrant, Co-Founder, iNLPCenter.org

As a psychotherapist I recognize how the work Mari is doing is not only helping so many individuals but contributing to the growth of the modern field of positive psychology, which I am a student of. As Mari writes in "Heal Yourself with Journaling Power," journal writing has 'moved from being an interesting "boutique" topic to a full-blown revolution.' It is part of this holistic wellness and positive psychology revolution which, in my opinion, is sorely needed

Paul B. Schlosberg, M.S. M.A. Professional Counselor and Wellness Coach

Dedication

To Bernie Sanders, who ignited my soul.

To Louise, my mother who art in heaven,

for her love and lunacy.

"A man's reach should exceed his grasp,

or what's a heaven for?"

—Robert Browning

"When I change the way I look at me,

the me I look at changes."

—Mari L. McCarthy

Foreword

Dennis Palumbo, M.A., MFT, Author and Psychotherapist

In the world of writing, I occupy what some might say is a very interesting space. Formerly a Hollywood screenwriter (the film MY FAVORITE YEAR; the TV series WELCOME BACK, KOTTER, etc.), I'm now a licensed psychotherapist in private practice in Los Angeles, specializing in creative issues. I'm also the author of a series of mystery thrillers whose protagonist, trauma expert Daniel Rinaldi, is himself a therapist.

As you might expect, my writing career and therapy practice have brought me into contact with a lot of interesting people. Mari L. McCarthy, the author of this compelling, informative book, is one of those people.

I've long been a believer in the healing power of expressive writing. So when Mari and the wonderful work she's been doing came to my attention, I could tell from her passion and dedication that she was going to help a lot of people...as, indeed, she has.

With her new book, *Heal Yourself with Journaling Power*, I know Mari is going to expand her reach, and bring her special knowledge and insight to even more people. You or someone you know may be one of them. Reading Mari's new book, you'll learn how to access the significant emotional truths derived from maintaining a consistent journaling routine.

I can say from my own experience—both personally and professionally—that there are tremendous therapeutic benefits to journaling. Writing about your thoughts and feelings does more than simply help clarify them.

Whenever you *write* a sentence, you simultaneously *read* that sentence. And when you read the sentence, you're sparked to ponder the thought or feeling behind it. This creates a healthy internal dialogue with yourself. It's always helpful to ask yourself questions about what you're doing, how you're feeling, and what those feelings mean. Journal writing is a very good way to do this. When you're doing it right, journaling should be more about writing and less about thinking. Words should be flowing from your innermost being, moment to moment, and impulse to impulse.

The beauty of journal writing is that it doesn't need to be structured. In fact, being unstructured makes it feel as though it's simply thinking on paper. Journaling should be like following the cascade of your thoughts as they are coming together, an experience that can run the gamut from inspiring to challenging. But almost always enlightening.

The most important value of expressive writing is that it's a private, spontaneous conversation with yourself. There are people who write journal entries that are meant to be published someday, while others just write them for themselves. I tend to favor the latter approach. I think that when you journal just for yourself, you're at your most authentic.

When you write privately and spontaneously—especially when you ask questions—answers seem to materialize, unsolicited, by way of your intuition. In fact, a big value of journaling is discovering that the answers to most of your questions are already inside you.

Another great benefit of journaling is that you have the freedom to just "follow your nose," allowing yourself to be guided to wherever your writing is taking you. When you do this regularly, it begins to feel like automatic writing, a process wherein there's little conscious intent. It's almost like you're taking dictation from someone, from your innermost self, and you're writing as fast as you can to keep up.

In my own journaling, I'm sometimes struck by how much emotion I'm carrying inside about a particular issue, whether relating to love, fear, anger, envy, or unresolved guilt. I consider this increased self-awareness to be perhaps the most important gift that journaling bestows.

The author Samuel Johnson once said, "Adversity introduces a man to himself." Likewise, I think journaling introduces a man or a woman to themselves—to who they really are, what they really think and feel. And, believe me, sometimes we can have a strong or complicated reaction to this person we're being introduced to!

Nevertheless, nearly all of us who journal come to realize that most of the issues we deal with every day remain the same. So it never surprises me when people tell me they've just read their journal from five years ago, and that, to their surprise, they sound pretty much like the same person.

That said, journaling strengthens and broadens your perspective, so that over time you come from a place of more wisdom or awareness about yourself and your issues. But the issues remain the same, and that's okay. *It's the understanding and perspective you've gained through journaling about your issues that counts.*

I believe that the self-knowledge, solace, and emotional clarity you'll gain through *Heal Yourself with Journaling Power* will be immense. Whether you've never journaled before, or else have a well-established journaling routine, the insights you'll derive from this thought-provoking book will help you through the challenging and introspective journey we call life.

* * *

Dennis Palumbo, M.A., MFT, is a writer and a licensed psychotherapist in private practice, specializing in creative issues. His newest crime novel, HEAD WOUNDS, is on sale now from Poisoned Pen Press. The book is the fifth in the series featuring psychologist and trauma expert Daniel Rinaldi.

Dennis Palumbo's credits as a former Hollywood screenwriter include the feature film My Favorite Year, for which he was nominated for a WGA Award for Best Screenplay. He was also a staff writer for the ABC-TV comedy series Welcome Back, Kotter, and he has written numerous TV series episodes and pilot scripts. You can learn more about Dennis and his writing at www.dennispalumbo.com.

Introduction

Join the Revolution!

A lot has changed since my first book, *Journaling Power,* which chronicled my personal story and summarized much of the published literature that substantiates the ability of expressive writing to heal numerous health ailments.

> The amazing power of journaling has moved from being an interesting "boutique" topic to a full-blown revolution!

Thousands of people around the world have discovered it, and more and more people are tapping into it every day. For good reason.

Illnesses are being mitigated, dreams are being realized, new talents are being discovered, self-limiting barriers are being smashed, people are healing themselves, and lives are being transformed. All through the unlimited power of pen-to-paper journaling.

Twenty years ago, I lost the feeling and function in the right side of my body. Multiple Sclerosis (MS) took them from me. The doctors weren't really helping, so I began a journey to take control of my health. After doing some research, I tried a writing therapy known as *Journaling for the Health of It.*

It wasn't easy for me. I had to learn to write with my left hand. But I dedicated myself to daily ACTION and began a journaling practice known as *Morning Pages*. I never could have anticipated how powerful this process would become. For nearly 20 years I've used the healing power of transformative journaling to…

- Improve my health…
- Generate business success, and…
- Create positive change in many areas of my life

My mission in life, and the purpose of ***Heal Yourself with Journaling Power***, is to help you mimic my success and reap the same rewards I did as quickly as possible. The truth is, I am a roaring testament to what numerous medical studies conclude: *journaling enhances life!*

The Benefits of Journaling Are Limitless

The power of journaling has impacted and inspired thousands of people worldwide. This is evident to me based on the fact that so many of my mentoring clients tell me stories about how journaling has helped them achieve clear-cut results in their lives, and how they now feel their possibilities are limitless.

I am pleased to share several of these stories in ***Heal Yourself with Journaling Power.***

Remember, ANYONE can journal. All you need for success is a resolve to journal every day! Yes, it's work, but it pays off if you're bold enough to MAKE IT HAPPEN!

In ***Journaling Power,*** I illustrated clearly how conventional medical wisdom has now fully embraced what I've been shouting to the world for years.

Expressive journaling has undeniable life-changing health benefits!

This absolute truth is supported by my life experience and numerous published studies in peer-reviewed medical journals. All of them substantiate the premise that putting pen to paper unleashes a healing agent that invigorates every cell in your body.

A 2012 review published in the *British Journal of General Practice* notes…

> *"Writing therapy can potentially help 30% of patients who visit primary care settings…"*

A published journal review in *Advances in Psychiatric Treatment* concludes…

> *"For some people expressive writing is extremely helpful and has quickly resolved issues that have been mulled over—sometimes for years—with no resolution."*

Many U.S. studies echo these conclusions, as do the heartfelt words of those who share their real-world stories in **Heal Yourself with Journaling Power**. Woven into these stories are the thoughts and findings of respected authorities on expressive writing that include:

- Dr. Joe Tatta, DPT, CNS
- Dennis Palumbo, M.A., MFT
- Jenetta Haim, Founder of Stressfree Management®

There is no longer any debate. Science and respected experts around the world confirm that journaling improves your life in numerous ways. The personal stories in this book are a treasure that I know will inspire you.

However, maybe you're impatient. Maybe you'd like to know right out of the gate what my top five reasons are to COMMIT to a daily journaling program immediately. Well, here they are:

Reason #1 – Reduce Stress

Writing about anger, sadness, and other painful emotions helps you release the intensity of these emotions. It promotes problem-solving and makes you feel calm. And, since stress is a major contributor to weight gain, chronic illness, insomnia, and loss of libido, journaling can radically shift your current reality.

Reason #2 – Relieve Physical Pain

Recording the details of your pain can uncover contributors like side effects from medication, environmental triggers, and emotional duress. Recognizing these patterns can help you minimize or avoid pain altogether. In addition, the emotional and health improvements journaling provides work to naturally diminish pain.

Reason #3 – Heal Inner Conflicts

Writing about the ups and downs of your daily life can provide perspective and allow you to learn valuable lessons. Studies show that writing your thoughts down helps you release them and free yourself from any negative impact they may be having on you. Tossing the pages you've written into the trash afterward can even signal your mind to toss away any limiting beliefs.

Reason #4 – Improve Relationships

Writing about disagreements instead of stewing over them helps you understand another's point of view. It also allows you to gain clarity about people who are toxic to you, so you can release them and develop new, healthy, satisfying relationships.

Reason #5 – Boost Memory and Comprehension

Composing your thoughts and ideas causes the mind to engage in cognitive recall – which hardwires information in your mind and increases your ability to remember. Exercises that involve cognitive recall have been shown to prevent or reduce the symptoms of diseases like Alzheimer's.

I can sum up these points by sharing with you one of my favorite expressions:

Journaling really can resolve the issues in your tissues!

For me personally, journaling brought me back from sick, tired, and downtrodden to healthy, full of life, joyful, and prosperous!

It wasn't easy. It required energy and massive action. But if you're reading this book, I know you're the type of person who believes in doing what it takes to make great strides in your life.

I want you to experience the SAME TRANSFORMATION I have. My commitment to you through this book is to...

- Put you on a path to better health and wellness
- Fill you with uplifting positive energy
- Give you the inspiration and motivation to keep going
- Introduce you to targeted journaling to help solve your most pressing problems

If you're ready to roll up your sleeves and get to work, you CAN overcome ANY obstacle. Take advantage of the power of journaling and write your way into the life of your dreams.

It takes work and commitment, but there is no denying this absolute fact: pen-to-paper journaling is a powerful tool you can use to heal yourself and manifest the life YOU want.

Lessons and Stories from Fellow Revolutionaries

Heal Yourself with Journaling Power goes beyond my first book, *Journaling Power*, by sharing amazing stories that are told by just a few of the thousands of people who have joined this revolution.

You'll discover the life-changing magic of journaling through their moving personal stories. They're all people just like you and me. As you'll soon discover, their challenges are the same ones you and I have.

Through them, you'll come to realize that your life is not "out there" somewhere, but that, rather, it's inside you. And you'll discover the unstoppable power of living your life from *the inside out.*

It will become crystal clear that you can use journaling as a tool to manifest everything you want. You'll realize that life is about *you*, and that you have the opportunity...and responsibility...to grow, expand, and heal yourself.

There has never been a better time than now to tap into this incredible power that is right at your fingertips. Why? Because you're not alone in this endeavor. In fact, you're surrounded by fellow revolutionaries who feel the same higher calling you do.

As I noted earlier, you're also going to hear from some amazing and authentic professionals who believe in the healing power of expressive writing.

Most important, they believe in holistic healing. They see you as a whole person, and not just a bucket full of symptoms that need to be treated with pills.

Every day there are more and more physicians, functional medicine specialists, and homeopaths who are leveraging the power of journaling to treat the mind, body, and soul, and to get to the root cause of your challenges. Their ranks are growing, and these incredible professionals are an important part of our revolution.

Lastly, each chapter includes a writing prompt that relates to the lessons taught and the stories told in every chapter.

> The purpose of each writing prompt is to inspire you to grab a pen and a pad and start writing!

Create the Life YOU Want

As you read, you'll awaken to how people from all walks of life have used pen-to-paper journaling to experience a personal transformation that takes them from self-sabotage to self-acceptance, self-love, and self-empowerment.

You'll realize that when you clear away the clutter and connect with your true self from the inside out, it's much easier to envision and create the life YOU want and deserve!

We really are souls having a human experience. Our purpose here is to be the best we can be.

Your life should be magical! It should be about unleashing your true talents, and growing, nurturing, and developing them continually.

Journaling is a life-changing tool you can use to make this tremendous change in your life. All it takes is a pen and paper, and a commitment. So why wait? Join the revolution and get started right now!

#WriteON!

> "No one else is going to see your journal, so just write. You can write in there whatever you want and then hide it under your bed if you wish. You can swear in your journal, you can write your secret dreams in your journal. The point is, when you journal you're getting it out, so you are no longer like a human pressure cooker."

—**Jenetta Haim**, Founder of Stressfree Management®;
Lifestyle and Health Management Expert

Chapter 1

Commit and Take Daily Action

It has now been 20 years since I first started journaling. I believe that things happen for a reason, and I know with certainty I was meant to discover the natural healing power of journaling and share it with the world.

However, I could not have anticipated the path I would travel to meet up with my destiny. But it certainly worked out the way it was supposed to.

In what seems like a lifetime ago, I was a highly successful business consultant. I routinely crisscrossed the country to provide solutions to a who's who of Fortune 1000 companies. I was constantly on the go, very energized, and I didn't give a whole lot of thought to what was going on inside me. I was busy, I had a lot to do, and my body and brain were simply the tools I needed to get things done.

However, at the height of my career I was forced to shut it all down due to the ravaging effects of Multiple Sclerosis (MS). In my first book, *Journaling Power*, I detailed the amazing story of how journaling reversed my debilitating MS symptoms and allowed me to ditch the lousy prescription-drug routine my doctors had put me on forever.

You may or may not have read *Journaling Power*, but either way, some of the highlights of my story are worth repeating.

In 1991 I was diagnosed with MS, which is a degenerative disease that affects nerve cells in the brain and the spinal cord. However, it affects everyone differently. At the time of my diagnosis, I could not predict the journey that lay before me.

All I knew was that that there was no known cause or cure.

By 1998, I didn't have the strength to cook a meal without dropping stuff all over the kitchen floor, and I had little function in the right side of my body. Bottom line: I had been floored by an ongoing health crisis.

I was forced to sell my consulting business, and I couldn't even write my name properly because I had lost the use of my right hand.

In the past I would routinely walk for miles for fun and fitness. Growing up, I was an exceptional sprinter and basketball player. So I was used to being on the go and being active.

However, now I could no longer walk down the street in a straight line, which made me look like the town drunk. I was devastated because I had always been the one who solved everyone else's problems.

Now I had to solve MY problem. And it was a big one!

In a desperate bid to recover my health I was walking in lockstep with conventional thinking. This means...you guessed it...I was taking a cocktail of prescription drugs every day as I dutifully went from one specialist to another.

But the pills didn't make me better. They made me worse.

It took a mammoth effort every day just to coordinate my legs and walk from the bedroom to the bathroom. Did I feel diminished by my chronic illness? Yeah, in a big way, and I wasn't happy about it.

I knew I needed a radical transformation. As I've said, I believe things happen for a reason, and I believe the Universe sends you messages. And it when it does, you'd better listen.

My message came to me through a friend who introduced me to writing therapy (also known as therapeutic journaling or expressive writing).

At first, I saw journaling as a means to an end. And that end was learning to write with my left hand, because my right hand was barely working.

However, as I began to write...a lot...I noticed that it eased my MS symptoms—especially when I wrote about them from the heart, with depth and honest emotion.

As I continued my writing practice, my MS symptoms improved. This made me want to write more. "Aha," I thought. I was on to something! This got my motor running and my determination grew by the week, and then the day, and then the hour!

I decided I wouldn't be stopped.

Through journaling I began to uncover, discover, and recover my True Self. I even tapped into talents I never knew I had. My personal transformation is nothing short of radical. Due to the power of journaling…

- The right side of my body is now 75 percent functional
- I take ZERO prescription drugs, and haven't for 13 years
- I stopped all over-the-counter medications eight years ago
- I dumped my health insurance and I haven't needed it for over 13 years
- I've been 100 percent healthy for six years, with no sign of *any* illness

It's quite a leap from my prognosis all those years ago. And it all happened because I made the decision to just go for it!

To be honest, I've found the benefits of a focused-journaling practice to be limitless. It has guided and supported me in making major dietary changes: no gluten, no dairy, and no processed foods.

I can write with both hands now, and thanks to my daily commitment to journaling, I routinely sleep through the night for seven or eight hours.

My energy increases each day. And my journal and I are currently working hard to accomplish my long-term goal, which is to heal myself for good!

Write Your Way to the Life of Your Dreams Starting Today!

Every day, I use the exact same journaling skills I now teach to create my perfect life. I live in a gorgeous beachfront home in Boston. And I have the freedom, flexibility, and physical ability to indulge in all my passions.

These days you'll find me writing, singing, reading, walking my beach, meditating, practicing photography, enjoying organic dark chocolate, cheering on the Pittsburgh Steelers, and raising roses and consciousness!

I literally created ALL of this with journaling power, and now I live life on MY terms!

Before uncovering my true self, I didn't even acknowledge my passion for music. I'd never dreamed I could become a singer. Well, goodbye to limits. In 2015 I released my third album, *Lady with a Song*. And I'm currently working on my fourth album, *Well-Written Songs*.

As you might expect, my journey to singing and making music sprang from my daily journaling practice.

In the winter of 1974, I was setting my sights on moving out of Pittsburgh. My first love, the captain of the Duquesne U baseball team, pitcher "Fast" Eddie Fritzky, ended "Us" and told me he wanted his baseball jacket back.

The breakup didn't faze me but giving him his baseball jacket back was not only gut-wrenching, but the only regret I've ever had in my life. What can I say, I liked the jacket.

Anyway, no sooner had I closed the front door than a song came on KQV by a new singer named Barry Manilow. The song title of course was *Mandy*, but all I heard was Mari. I thought how cool, I just accomplished another goal: having a guy write a song just for me.

When I got into journaling and rediscovered my love for music and my desire to become a real singer, I set a goal of meeting Barry Manilow, so I could thank him for inspiring me (*Yes he felt sad when I was sad, etc.*).

Anyway, the universe presented me the opportunity in 2004. Not only did I get to meet Mr. Manilow, but I also got to read him my poem "Since Forever." I told him one day I would turn it into a song, and he hugged me.

This is just one of my many "journaling accomplishments." However, my most fulfilling accomplishment of all is sharing my knowledge with people like you. I really hope you won't wait another minute to begin your amazing journey.

Don't put it off. Today could be the day that completely changes your life, so don't let this incredible opportunity pass you by. Because right now, at this moment, you have at your fingertips a secret power that is PROVEN to help you...

- Reduce stress and physical pain
- Overcome illness and other life challenges
- Heal emotional wounds from past traumas
- Resolve inner conflicts and improve relationships
- Gain a deeper understanding of your true authentic self
- Conquer limiting beliefs and fears that have held you back
- Create the life you want from the inside out!

Take action, make a commitment, and just go for it. If you're not sure what angle or approach to take with your journal writing, just keep reading. The stories, lessons, and journal prompts throughout this book from people just like you will give you a multitude of ideas.

Nothing Special About Me. I Just Did It. You Can Too.

As I stated earlier, it has been 20 years since I started journaling. It all began when I discovered a book by Emily Hanlon called *The Art of Fiction Writing*. It was through this book that I learned about having an inner critic.

Prior to reading *The Art of Fiction Writing*, I wasn't aware I had an inner critic. I just thought I was nuts! However, Emily Hanlon, in her infinite wisdom, made me realize I was normal, and that I didn't need an exorcism. Thank you, Emily!

My point here is that there is nothing special about me. I just made a commitment to expressive journaling, and it changed my life. Through my daily journaling practice, I have learned to manage my life, as opposed to letting outside forces manipulate me. Instead of reacting to external things and events coming at me, I use journaling to co-create the life I want.

I now know who I am, and I am in charge of my life. From a spiritual and emotional point of view, this is the biggest change I've made. I've been able to do this because journaling has allowed me to work through all the *issues in my tissues* from my childhood.

It no longer pains me anymore to speak my mind. From a physical point of view, I feel very good because I'm in tune with my spirituality, my emotions, and my mentality, as well as my physicality.

I am entering my fifteenth year without using prescription drugs, and as a result my health continues to improve. As for non-prescription pills, I can also say proudly that I am now in my tenth year without any *over-the-counter craziness* in my life.

I have not carried health insurance for many years because I no longer saw the point of paying $8,000 to $10,000 a year on the off chance that something is going to happen to me. Especially when insurance doesn't cover anything that is going to help me stay healthy. *I'm not saying everyone should drop their health insurance, but it has worked out well for me.*

Gain Clarity

In addition to amazing health benefits, journaling has brought tremendous clarity to my life.

I now realize that when I was on medication, it was because I had given into the head games the traditional medical system was pushing on me. We all need to take responsibility for the fact that at times in our lives we have allowed conventional doctors and the medical system to play God Almighty in our lives without really questioning what we were being "sold."

We must take responsibility for our own health and wellness experience, just like we take responsibility for the health of our pets, and the condition of our cars and appliances. After all, nothing is more important than our physical and mental health, so why on Earth should we blindly delegate this responsibility to someone else?

I can tell you through my experience with MS that your health is definitely something you can take charge of through journaling. Journaling can be essential to making lifestyle changes, forming healthier habits, taking command of your life, and creating your destiny.

Journaling helped me realize that when it came to my health I was as much of a "hamster on the wheel" as anyone else. I was guilty of buying into the latest new drugs that were going to "hopefully kind of maybe help" mitigate my MS symptoms. And with any luck, the side effects wouldn't be too unbearable.

Who wants to live like that? I sure don't.

Journaling helped me dig into my thought processes, so I could realize what a bunch of crap I was being sold. I realized that if the medical establishment doesn't know what causes MS…and they don't have a cure… what's a drug really going to do for me other than allow me to be a human vehicle that makes pharmaceutical companies rich, while I deal with mind-numbing side effects?

Through journaling, I discovered my health was better served by making nutritional lifestyle changes. It was all about embracing change, and journaling helped me get to the core of my life, so I could view my "whole picture" more clearly.

I got away from the grind of being just another person who accepted the notion of "That's the way we've always done things." Journaling made me aware that like millions of other people, I had just given in to the medical establishment and walked in lockstep with what they told me to do, while they made money from it.

Think about it. Do you think you'll ever hear about the proven, documented benefits of journaling from a pharmaceutical company or the conventional medical companies? Of course you won't. Why not?

Because journaling is free! You can do it yourself and heal and transform your life.

Does starting a life-changing journaling practice require you to get out of your comfort zone? You bet it does. But you can do this. You just have to commit to it. A quote attributed to Ralph Waldo Emerson states…

"Once you make a decision, the Universe conspires to make it happen."

There's Only One Way to Journal. YOUR Way!

If you can write a shopping list, you can journal. In fact, I'll take it a step further and say with complete conviction that there's only one way to way to journal—and that's YOUR way!

Never forget this.

Just put pen to paper and let your natural voice pour forth as if you're having a conversation with your best friend.

Proper grammar? Who cares! You don't have to turn your journal in to a teacher to be graded. Sloppy handwriting? Join the club. As long as *you* can read your journal, you're fine. So relax. Have fun and don't hold back. Just be yourself.

Again, if you can write a shopping or to-do list, you have all the talent it takes to transform your mind, health, and soul through journaling.

Plus, throughout *Heal Yourself with Journaling Power* you will get extensive advice, wisdom, and instruction from several people who just sat their butts down in a chair and got busy.

You'll read about their routines, learn their stories, and discover the mental tools they use to experience a lifelong voyage of physical and emotional empowerment.

> *"Get in the habit of writing something every single day. Even if you write that you don't feel like writing…you're writing! This may motivate you to add a sentence or two—and next thing you know, you're off and running. The goal with journaling can be to simply get your thoughts and feelings out. Repressing them can lead to emotional problems and physical ailments."*

—**Jenetta Haim**, Founder of Stressfree Management®;
Lifestyle and Health Management Expert

Reconnect with Your Core, Your Center, and Your True Authentic Self

As you read and explore *Heal Yourself with Journaling Power*, it will become evident to you that the road to self-love, peace, and inner security can be paved with a pen.

The wonderful stories you'll read in this book, coupled with scientific evidence, support the revelation that expressive journaling can facilitate personal transformation through which you…

- Let go of hang-ups and disempowering thoughts that hold you back
- Elevate feelings of joy and lightness while reducing depression
- Feel gratitude for the present moment and forgive past missteps
- Tap into power, talents, and abilities you've previously denied
- Commit to new goals and take inspired actions to achieve them
- Participate in the curing of your own disease!

Think about this: your fingertips give you the ability to pick up prescription pills and pop them in your mouth. But this doesn't have to be what you do to feel better!

The stories and lessons in this book will show you exactly how to use those same fingertips to leverage

a holistic power that has a magnificent healing effect on your mind and body.

The best part? Journaling can heal YOU without the nasty side effects of those pills you've been conditioned to take!

The Lesson in All This

There is nothing wrong with putting YOU at the center of the universe. The people you see on the news, in the movies, and on your favorite sports teams are not more important than you.
Your life is about you!

Focus on what YOU want. Keep your mind centered on YOUR dreams and YOUR desires. Tony Robbins frequently says, "What you focus on expands." This is incredibly simple, but true.

Create the exact life you want—by writing about the life you want, the health you want, and the relationships you want.

Is this a selfish way to look at life? No, it's not. Here's why.

When you realize your dreams and create the life you want, you are in a much more powerful position to help other people and be of service to them, and to donate more money to charities.

Think about it. Before Tony Robbins was able to help millions of people around the world, he first became the best possible version of Tony Robbins.

Before Oprah Winfrey inspired people around the globe, she first became her ultimate version of what she knew Oprah Winfrey could be. You can say the same thing about any number of people you respect and admire.

So put yourself first and love yourself!

Your Journaling Prompt

You will be given journaling prompts at the end of each chapter in this book. Some of these prompts will be in the form of very specific journaling exercises. However, this first one is very global in nature. And, it is this:

Commit to a daily pen-to-per journaling practice right now—
and start writing!

All you need is a pen and a yellow pad, or slips of paper, or a nice-looking journal filled with blank pages that you buy at the store. It's your choice. Just start writing about…

- An ailment you are determined to overcome
- Emotional pain you want to cast from your life
- Relationships that you need to release and put behind you
- Goals you're going to accomplish no matter what gets in your way
- The new life story you're going to tell yourself each and every day
- The things you absolutely love about yourself that you take for granted

Write about anything you want. The key is to just start writing. The tone and theme of your journal can always change and evolve over time. So you don't need to over-prepare.

Just commit and do it! Again, all you need is a pen and paper. The beauty of this simple system is that you DON'T have to…

- Buy and learn software
- Deal with power surges or outages
- Worry about being hacked

- Become a techie
- Connect a bunch of equipment together

All you have to do is grab a pen, get your hands on some paper, and get after it!

When you were young, you may have been told to get off your butt and do something. But I'm giving you permission to sit on your butt and journal!

Remember, your life is about you, not the rest of the world. So commit and start your journaling practice today.

Heal Yourself with Journaling Power is loaded with inspiring ideas about how you can set up and organize your journaling. So keep reading and get busy!

"The most important value of expressive writing is that it is a private, spontaneous conversation with yourself. When you write just for yourself, you are at your most authentic."

—Dennis Palumbo, M.A., MFT,
Author and Psychotherapist

Chapter 2

Launch a Healthy Life

If you know anything about my story, you know I am a living, breathing example of how pen-to-paper journaling has the PROVEN healing power to help you beat back physical ailments. In my case, Multiple Sclerosis symptoms.

Create Write Now tribe member Jenny Patton is another shining example of how expressive writing can heal and transform your mind, body, and spirit. Jenny began journaling on legal pads when she was a seven-year-old girl. As you might expect, her initial journey into journaling began with writing about what boys she had a crush on, and which girls were mean to her at school.

And then she experienced what we call fear.

She lost her journal, and the older brothers of the boy across the street found it…and read it aloud to him in front of her. After they read it aloud, they threw it down the stairs at Jenny, and the boy she had a crush on kindly handed it to her before she ran home, mortified.

This of course was traumatic for young Jenny. However, Jenny loved journaling, so for her eighth birthday she got a journal with a lock and key and persisted with her writing!

Jenny continued to journal on and off again through college when she had important issues to deal with. However, after college she dropped her journaling routine for the most part until she was thirty-four. It was during this time in her life that a series of events began to merge, which inspired Jenny to turn back to journaling.

Her mother was dying of cancer, she had an addict in her life she was trying to save from himself, and she was wrestling with the reality that her son had been diagnosed with autism. In addition, Jenny was working as a stringer for a local newspaper and she worked mostly nights doing odd assignments, even though she was a morning person by nature.

Juggling all of these challenges put tremendous stress and strain on Jenny, which slowly drained her energy and health. She soon developed Crohn's disease, extreme joint pain, and a variety of other ailments. In the course of trying to treat them, Jenny came to the realization that many of her physical problems were interconnected.

This is when her intuition guided her back to her journaling practice, which she combined with prayer, meditation, and yoga.

Rediscovering journaling empowered Jenny to have deep conversations with herself. She also learned through her writing exploration that journaling taps into the problem-solving portion of your brain.

Perhaps most important, Jenny says she discovered that "Your friends want to give you advice. Your journal doesn't. It just listens."

After her mother passed from her battle with cancer, Jenny found she was able to continue her conversation with her through journaling. Overall, journaling helped Jenny rediscover herself, and it helped her realize what really matters most to her. It also helped her reinforce what her intuition told her she needed to be doing.

Jenny summarized her journaling journey beautifully in a blog post that she was kind enough to share with our Create Write Now tribe. I find it to be very inspiring, so I want to share it with you here.

My Launching Pad to a Healthy Life

By Jenny Patton

When I was seven, I made my own journal out of legal pad paper—a little book that sparked a passion for writing down my thoughts, feelings and desires. E.M. Forster asks, "How do I know what I think until I see what I say?" Here's my take: "How do I know who I am until I see what I think?"

Even though I knew how much journaling helped me make decisions, solve problems and reflect on the person I was becoming, I let life—work, kids, other responsibilities—take over and didn't journal during most of my twenties. During those years, I developed endometriosis, tendinitis, Crohn's disease, osteoarthritis and other autoimmune illnesses.

In my early thirties, after my mom died, my Crohn's disease flared up and I dropped to ninety pounds, unable to digest food normally. I made mistakes at work, snapped at my children and avoided my friends. I wanted to curl up in a ball and stay in bed. But each winter morning, I lit a candle, practiced yoga and wrote in my journal—which became a way to coach myself back to health.

Although I didn't know it then, journal writing has been proven to combat stress and help treat eating disorders, depression, addiction and other psychologically rooted problems. And people who write about past traumas show stronger immune systems.

With more awareness of my behavior and how it affected my health, I realized how much a dairy-free, gluten-free diet and a well-paced life benefited me. I no longer needed Remicade infusions and other medications to keep my autoimmune illnesses at bay.

Soon I renewed my friendships, enrolled in graduate school and embarked on a new career—all goals I set and fulfilled with the help of daily journal writing.

Now that I'm in my forties, my morning journal-writing practice still fuels my days. It's also given me the confidence to share the benefits of journaling with college students, wellness-coaching clients and community members at journaling workshops and yoga-writing workshops as well as through a blog read by people around the world.

* * *

Jenny Patton teaches writing at The Ohio State University, works as a Mayo Clinic-certified wellness coach and is a registered yoga instructor. At www.journalingwithjenny.blogspot.com, she posts journal prompts designed to help people learn more about themselves and become who they want to be. To receive prompts by email, contact journalingwithjenny@gmail.com or @JournalWJenny.

Ask Yourself for Advice First

Jenny Patton teaches writing at THE Ohio State University, and her students often use her office hours to ask her for advice on a variety of issues that impact young college students. Typically, the life issues facing her students revolve around the questions "Should I do this?" or "Should I do that?"

Rather than trying to play Dr. Phil, like many professors might, Jenny usually gives her students an on-the-spot journaling exercise. She simply has them journal for 10 minutes on their different options. When the exercise is completed, Jenny's students usually tell her that they now know exactly what to do!

This is one of the amazing benefits of honest journaling.

When you commit your "should I?" or "could I?" questions to paper, the answers you seek will come flying back to you through your intuition. This is because the answers you're looking for are almost always already within you. Journaling just draws them out into the open so you can see and feel them.

How convenient is that?

So when you need to ask someone for heartfelt advice, ask YOURSELF first through your journal. When you do, you'll be pleasantly surprised to learn things about yourself you didn't know you already knew!

Greater Clarity and More Certainty

The tremendous benefit of asking yourself for advice through your journal is the clarity and certainty you'll feel when your answers come to you through your intuition, inner voice, or gut instinct (whatever YOU choose to call it).

Think about it. How many times have you asked friends for advice and then walked away from the ensuing conversation only to feel more confused than before you talked to them?

If you're like me, you've been through this drill many times. That's because "advice" conversations with friends and family tend to revolve around what you "should" do. However, when you have a conversation with yourself through your journal, it will revolve more around what you "could" do. This will lead to your inner voice telling you what you WANT to do.

When you know what you WANT to do, you'll feel a rush of clarity and certainty and your intuition will fill your being with actions you can take to support your "want."

And as I've said before, it's OK to WANT things for yourself.

The bottom line is this: journaling leads to more clarity and more certainty in who you are and what you want. It takes you inward and gives you a grounding and a sense of self that feels natural to you.

Journaling and Your Health—Jenny Patton's Take

I have written in the first chapter of this book, and extensively in my book *Journaling Power*, about the incredible effects journaling has had on my health.

In preparing to write *Heal Yourself with Journaling Power*, it was important to me to include the stories of others who have used the power of journaling to overcome physical ailments. This is what motivated me to have a nice discussion with Jenny Patton about the blog post she wrote for CreateWriteNow.com, which serves as the foundation for this chapter.

After our talk, Jenny sent me a very thoughtful follow-up email about the impact journaling has had on her health. As I read it, I realized it was a very nice sequel to her blog post. After reading it several more times, my thought was, "This is wonderful; I definitely want to incorporate Jenny's additional thoughts from her email into this chapter."

I then spent a little time contemplating the best way to do this. I read her email one more time and realized it was essentially a blog post in itself. So I concluded the best way to include the thoughts from her email into this chapter was to simply include her email in this chapter.

Pretty brilliant, wouldn't you say?

So with Jenny Patton's permission, here is an email she sent me that discusses the impact journaling has had on her health.

Mari L. McCarthy

Jenny's email

Hi Mari,

If I may, I'd like to expand on my thoughts about journaling and health. I often hesitate to tell people why I believe journaling has helped me heal, as the academic part of me anticipates sideways glances.

I'd long associated stress with heart disease, but in Louise Hay's book *You Can Heal Your Life,* she links negative thought patterns and limited beliefs with illness. This opened me up to the mind-body connection in a new way.

Hay links headaches to self-criticism, hip problems to a fear of moving forward, and cancer to deep hurt and longstanding resentment. And she offers healthy replacement thought patterns as part of the healing process.

In my experience, holding onto stress and/or emotional pain leads to illness. If our minds don't convince us to take action to change a situation—such as a relationship or job—or if we haven't yet worked through a past trauma, our bodies step in, often in a big way. My host of autoimmune issues—calcioarthritis, endometriosis, Crohn's disease, among others—forced me to stop, rest and reassess.

During the year in which my body gave out on me, I wrote and wrote as a way to process my mother's death, my son's autism-spectrum diagnosis, and my role in trying to help a loved one overcome a narcotic addiction. Journaling helped me interact with, and come to terms with, each of these life-altering events on a deep level—and to grow from my experiences. In turn, my physical body began to heal.

Back then I didn't know that studies had proven that people who wrote about trauma strengthened their immune cells, called T-lymphocytes, and had fewer health-center visits for six months after writing. What I did know was that I had to do something if I wanted things to be different, and journaling played a pivotal role in my recovery, along with yoga, meditation, diet changes, and a job shift.

And though I don't suffer from chronic back pain, I found the book *Healing Back Pain: The Mind-Body Connection* by Dr. John Sarno profound for the way he communicates the link between the mind and

38

body: "Mental and emotional states can impinge upon and alter, for good or ill, any of the body's organs or systems" (139). Here a Clinical Rehabilitation Medicine professor at the New York University School of Medicine expressed what I felt I'd experienced. After reading his book, in my journal I traced a lifetime's worth of injuries, accidents and illnesses to various forms of emotional distress.

Now when I hear that people are sick or injured, I pray not just for physical healing, but also for resolution of the underlying emotional event that I believe may have gotten them there. And, if appropriate, I encourage them to journal.

Mari, I hope you find these thoughts helpful as you write *Heal Yourself with Journaling Power*.

Best,

Jenny Patton

Yes, Jenny. I find your thoughts very helpful, and I am proud to include them in this book. Thank you so much for sharing this with our Create Write Now tribe!

The Lesson in All This

Nothing is more important to you than your health, so it is vital to understand that every cell in your body is affected by your thoughts and emotions. In fact, everything about your mind, body, and soul is interconnected.

You no doubt have heard or read about the staggering amount of evidence that links emotional stress to heart disease. This of course is a well-known dramatic example of how your emotional state can impact your health.

However, it's often easy to overlook how everyday negative thoughts and/or critical self-talk can impact your health on a less dramatic level. For example, your irritating lower back pain may be from excessive worrying about financial issues. Or perhaps you can attribute the joint pain and muscle tightness you feel every morning to stressing over workplace politics.

Everybody is different. Worrying and stressing about different issues may impact different areas of your mind, body, and spirit.

The lesson here is that what you worry about and stress over impacts your health and how your body feels. Instead of eating aspirin or taking prescription pills to deal with this pain, you may just want to grab your journal and start putting pen to paper.

It's a lot less expensive and you don't have to deal with nasty side effects.

Journaling affords you a great opportunity to confront your health issues head-on. It allows you to pour out your thoughts and feelings about your pain, and the issues in your life that are causing it. By confronting the issues in your tissues head on through your writing, you'll be able to RELEASE them instead of just *treating* them temporarily.

By being fully aware that your thoughts and emotions impact your body, you'll be motivated to make better choices when it comes to what you think about.

Consider this. If you are a health-conscious person, you're already aware that you need to be picky about what you eat. But to truly be a health-conscious person, you need to be equally picky about what you think!

Your Journaling Prompt

Using journaling as a launching pad to a healthier life can begin with a simple prompt. Grab your pen and pad and do this basic fill-in-the blanks exercise.

"When I think about _____, I feel really _____."

When you write down this prompt, your intuition will fuel your mind immediately with words to fill in the blanks. You may even be surprised at what pops up! It may be something deep, or it may be something on a surface level.

Whatever jumps to mind through this prompt will be something that is taking up space in your brain. This simple exercise will be a signal to you that it's time to deal with it and write about it.

When you fill in the "I feel really..." blank, you can ask yourself, "Why do I feel this way?" Answer this question by writing a few lines, a few paragraphs, or even a few pages. Then, ask yourself, "Why do I feel this way?" a second time and go into even greater detail.

By this point, your thoughts and feelings will be pouring out. Things that were buried deep within you will rise to the surface. They will be right in front of your face and there'll be no hiding from them in detail.

The result will be mental and physical relief!

So if you have aches and pains and problems (and we all do!) that have been lingering deep inside you, follow this basic journaling prompt...be honest with yourself...and run with it!

> "There are studies that show expressive writing is a good way to manage and alleviate stress. Journaling can decrease stress chemicals in your body. And if you have fewer stress chemicals, then you have less stress response in your body. This in turn can reduce your physical pain."
>
> —**Dr. Joe Tatta**, DPT, CNS

Chapter 3

Your No-Cost On-Call Therapist

Ever thought of spending a bunch of money on a therapist? I have an alternative solution that will save you a boatload of cash and get you all the answers you need.

My solution? You guessed it. Journaling.

If you have things on your mind about which you need to rant and rave (and who doesn't?), you're going to enjoy this chapter.

If you need answers or solutions to questions, challenges, obstacles, or things that have been flat-out annoying the heck out of you, you're going to love this form of journaling.

Let me start by asking you this question. In general, why would you consider going to a therapist to discuss the issues in your tissues?

Well, most likely you'd go to a therapist to open up and get things off your chest. In the privacy of a therapist's office you can rant and rave and say things you may not say to your friends, colleagues, or your family.

With a therapist you can just let it go and say anything you want. But would you really do this? You might tell a therapist a lot, but would you really tell her everything? Sure, you may open up and share 90% to 95% of your true feelings and innermost thoughts.

But if you're anything like me, there might be that five percent (or more!) that you'd feel too embarrassed or awkward about to share with anyone. And if you choose to open up and rant to a therapist, what do you really want from her in return?

Bottom line: you'd want answers. And not just general answers. You'd want very specific, definitive answers. Now consider that therapists charge you by the hour. And when I say by the hour, I mean probably more than $200 per hour.

Given that this is how therapists make a living, you have to ask this simple question: does a therapist have an incentive to give you the answers you seek quickly?

Of course not! Why? Because they charge by the hour. So they have a financial incentive to give you the answers you seek very slowly over multiple therapy sessions. And there's no guarantee that when they do give you answers they're going to be the right ones!

On top of all this, you may be among the very large group of people who believe that going to a therapist is another way of saying, "Hey, I think I might be nuts!"

I'm exaggerating with this example because I don't believe anyone who seeks therapy is nuts. Let's face it, we all have problems and we all could use some help from time to time. And there are definitely times when seeking out a professional therapist is your best course of action. I am fully supportive of the role professional therapists can play in helping you deal with pressing life issues.

However, we all have everyday issues in our tissues about which we need to rant and vent. Now, when I say rant and vent, I mean really turn it loose and let it go. And for this, I suggest turning to the least expensive and most honest therapist in town.

Her name is Dr. Journal.

If you have a pen and pad, Dr. Journal is always right at your fingertips, and Dr. Journal is always willing to listen. And if you're open and honest with your writing, Dr. Journal will always give you immediate feedback and answers—and Dr. Journal is always RIGHT!

So grab your journal, get strong, and let it all out. Be bold and be COURAGEOUS!

There are a tremendous benefits to courageous journaling. Before I detail them, I want to further set the stage by sharing a beautiful blog post Antoinette Truglio Martin wrote on this topic for our community. It is posted on CreateWriteNow.com, and I am pleased to publish it here as well.

Courageous Journaling

By Antoinette Truglio Martin

Originally, I began journaling as proof of my writing ambitions. I was a young teen—maybe younger. Marbled composition books, diaries with locks, and beautifully bound journals were cluttered with ramblings of story starters, poetry experiments, and quiet observations. I did not notice that my thoughts and heart were quietly affirmed. I just wrote—some days more than others.

Then cancer hit. Fear, anger, and doubt were cast front and center. Hearing and speaking the words shook me to the core, even though my prognosis that I'd survive Stage I breast cancer was excellent. But I needed to be brave, and courage was not in my skill set. I knew I had to stay connected and be supported by the people I loved without frightening them or myself.

I turned to journaling. I chose an ugly spiral notebook to rant, rage, complain and question. I had a private on-call therapist at the end of my pen. The quiet purging allowed me to practice the vocabulary and use the words to compose emails to my vast tribe of friends and family—My Everyone. My thoughts were cohesively ordered. My Everyone filled my heart with an outpouring of love and inclusion. I was not alone. Courage stealthily appeared and just like that, I began asking pertinent questions, speaking up for myself, and completing a course of treatment.

I had planned to go through the journal and emails a year after treatment. I thought it would be a good story complete with drama, whimsy, and a happy ending. But each time I revisited the pages, I got caught up in the horror. I hated feeling that fear again. Finally, I buried the evidence, secretly hoping to lose it all in the deep abyss of stuff.

Then, within five years, Stage IV cancer hit. Now the cancer is forever. The familiar fear, anger, and doubt crept back. I resurrected that ugly journal and compiled the emails into an accessible file. While reading through the entries, I was astounded at how brave I had become that year. It gave me hope and a compass to navigate this new diagnosis.

Today, cancer does not get a journal of its very own. There is too much life in my days and too many stories to tell to dedicate to one issue. Right now, treatment is not too debilitating nor intrusive to give cancer center stage. I am so very fortunate—so grateful. I continue to try to write daily in my journal. I complain, rant, and rage at will. It is not always about cancer. The on-call therapist is always open. My ramblings are, as always, filled with story starters, poetry experiments, and quiet observations. Gratitude is prevalent.

* * *

*Antoinette Truglio Martin is a speech therapist and special-education teacher by training, but she is a writer at heart. She is the author of the children's picture book **Famous Seaweed Soup** (Albert Whitman & Company) and was a visiting author in schools for several years.*

*Antoinette's memoir, **Hug Everyone You Know: A Year of Community, Courage, and Cancer**, was published in 2017. The book chronicles her first year of breast-cancer treatment as a wimpy patient. Her journal entries and email correspondences are featured prominently through the story.*

*In addition, Antoinette was formerly a regular columnist for **Parent Connection** (In A Family Way) and **Fire Island Tide** (Beach Bumming). Personal-experience essays and excerpts of her memoir were published in **Bridges**, **Visible Ink**, and **The Southampton Review**. She proudly received her MFA in creative writing and literature from Stony Brook Southampton University in 2016. As a Stage IV breast-cancer patient, she does not allow cancer to dictate her life. She lives in her hometown of Sayville, NY, with her husband, Matt.*

Visit her at https://antoinettetrugliomartin.com/ or on Facebook.

Be Bold and Loud

Whether you're dealing with health issues or other personal matters, courageous journaling gives you the opportunity to be bold, to be loud, and write down anything you want any way you want.

Remember, this is YOUR journal. Nobody is going to read it but you. You don't have to be polite with your writing, and you don't have to be politically correct. You can bring down the hammer and write anything YOU want that is bothering you.

Again, it's the best and least expensive form of therapy. When you write about things that upset you in a hard, direct manner, solutions will start flowing back to you in the form of answers and action plans.

The key is to be brutally honest with your thoughts. In other words, be courageous! This is a great way to get things out of your system that you might otherwise keep bottled up.

The tremendous benefit of courageous journaling is that it allows you to get the words out without anybody else hearing them. So you don't have to worry about filtering your thoughts, and you don't have to worry about "saying things" to someone that you later feel the need to amend or apologize for.

This is an incredible tool when you have fierce issues going on in your life. We all know people who've kept quiet about what was eating them up inside, until one day they let loose and exploded with rage and anger they later felt embarrassed about.

Now, imagine if these people had instead emptied their rage and anger onto the pages of their journal. They'd feel so much relief inside, and they'd have absolutely nothing for which to apologize!

Have you known someone like this? More important, has this person ever been you? If it has, it never has to be again. Because now you can rant and rave whenever you need to...to Dr. Journal!

Are you angry with your boss or a co-worker? Let 'em have it in your journal. Rant and rave and spill your guts about how you really feel. Let it all out!

Are you angry because you're struggling with health issues? Pour your raw, honest thoughts into your journal. Remember, Dr. Journal is there to listen to you 24/7, and she doesn't charge a dime.

Everybody gets angry and upset. It's part of being human. What sets us apart is how we deal with it. We all know it's never healthy to keep things bottled up, but it can be equally as unhealthy to explode emotionally and verbally rage in front of others.

On the other hand, verbally exploding into your journal can be courageous, combative, and incredibly cleansing! So go for it!

Collect and Organize Your Thoughts

When the issues in your tissues have you really worked up, there is a huge advantage to letting your rage loose on Dr. Journal, instead of flying off the handle during a personal confrontation.

When you have issues you know will eventually require a direct conversation with someone, journaling about them first gives you the advantage of being able to collect and organize your thoughts. It also enables you to rehearse the thoughts, feelings, and words you need to communicate.

The benefit of this process is that when you finally do confront someone with your issue, you won't come across as an over-emotional mess who is shooting from the hip with a series of rambling and disconnected thoughts.

Journaling your rants before an inevitable confrontation also gives you time to pause and consider someone else's point of view, or the other side of an issue you're dealing with. Over time this can deliver a sense of ease, calm, and healing to you.

Ranting and complaining to Dr. Journal also gives you a tremendous chance to fiddle with your feelings and thoughts over a period of days after your initial pen-to-paper outburst. By doing this, you are not continually dealing with your issues and the people connected to them in a state of emotional upheaval.

Think of times in your past when you had an issue with a friend, lover, co-worker, or family member that resulted in a confrontation where both of you got emotional, shot from the hip, and said things you later regretted. Or, as most often is the case, you *didn't* say things you wish you would have.

When you think back to these times (and we've all had many), wouldn't it have been a great advantage to you if you had at least a day or two to first rant to Dr. Journal? Wouldn't it have been a big help if you had first put your emotional rant on paper, and then taken a day or two to sort through your thoughts and feelings before you had a direct conversation with someone about the issue at hand?

Sure, there are some issues that confront us on the spur of the moment, and we have no choice but to react to and deal with them immediately. But the large majority of our issues are challenges we see coming ahead of time.

Spending some time venting to Dr. Journal (who doesn't charge a dime) is a great way to work through your challenges before they lead to a confrontation with someone.

Plus, you'll be in a much calmer, cooler state during your conversation, which can provide you with a big edge if you're confronting someone who's never heard of Dr. Journal.

Look Back on Your Rants and Learn

Courageous journaling gives you a fantastic way to write things down you might not want to say out loud. You don't have to be polite, proper, dignified, classy, or politically correct. You can just let it rip!

Not only CAN you do this, but it's important that you DO! Be brutally honest with your thoughts and feelings and let them pour out. The more honest you are with your writing, the more helpful Dr. Journal becomes.

When you are real and authentic with Dr. Journal, she will reward you by sending back answers, solutions, and action plans that are equally real, honest, and authentic.

In addition, when you are true and honest with Dr. Journal, you'll realize that all your thoughts and feelings have value. And when you commit them to paper you will truly realize this.

Then you will have the power to choose whether you want to express these thoughts and feelings publicly with one or several people. You will also be able to decide if you need to keep certain thoughts and feelings to yourself, and just learn from them.

Another benefit of being open and honest with your rants is that you can look back on them and learn. For example, when you read your courageous journal entries from six months or a year ago, you will notice things like...

- I've come so far in this past year because I learned so much from my rants.
- I notice I only half committed to the action plans I said I would take six months ago.
- I no longer hang out with the people who motivated my rants last year, and I've made new friends and I feel energized.

- Gee, I seem to be ranting about the same damn things as I was a year ago, and I'm hanging out with the same people and repeating the same old patterns. I need to get on the ball and address this!

This is a great example of why you shouldn't hesitate to rant your raw, unfiltered thoughts to Dr. Journal. Let's face it, they're in your head so you may as well write them down.

This way, when you look back in your journal you'll be able to see if your rants from a year ago are the same ones in your head right now. On the positive side, you'll also be able to see if last year's rants are a distant memory you've learned from and left in your past as you've moved on to bigger and better things.

The Lesson in All This

Courageous journaling is a great way to open up, let loose with your thoughts, get things out, and destress. It's a hell of a lot better than keeping things bottled up and allowing the stress to eat you up inside.

Courageous journaling is the perfect way to say things you may not want to say in front of other people. It's also a great way to write down the thoughts you have that nobody really wants to hear. In short, it's the perfect way to say anything you want to say without a filter.

And Dr. Journal is always willing to listen. She's available 24/7, her answers are always right, and she doesn't charge a damn thing!

Plus, you'll be amazed at what comes back to you from Dr. Journal when you have the courage to rant on paper in a way you never would out loud. Antoinette Truglio Martin tells me that what often comes back to her through her intuition are answers to her questions and challenges, and lists of action plans she should/could be executing.

A word about the word *should*. Try not to put too many *shoulds* on yourself, when the word *could* is so much more liberating. There are very few things you should do (you *should* take baths or showers and pay your taxes), but there is an endless list of things you *could* do.

The word *could* presents you with options, and we love having options. The word *could* takes you on a path on which you can get clear on what you really want. When we explore what we could do, it invites us to really get clear on what we WANT.

As you'll hear me say many times throughout this book, there's nothing wrong with WANTING something.

Your Journaling Prompt

As you might guess from reading this chapter, there is nothing too fancy or formal about starting a courageous journaling practice. But I am going to add a little twist.

Before you grab your pen and pad and start busting out your rants, take a few moments to journal about at least one good thing that happened to you in the last 24 hours.

By taking the time to express gratitude for at least one good thing that has happened to you, you'll avoid turning your journal into a complete and total negative rant-fest! And be just as open and courageous with your gratitude as you are your rants.

After you take some time to express your gratitude, then you can roll into your rants! Dr. Journal will always be there to listen, 24/7, and be your no-cost therapist. I truly believe this is an exceptional form of therapy for people who have a tough time opening themselves up and expressing themselves verbally.

When you journal your rants, be open to solutions and action plans flowing back to you through your intuition, and then commit to taking action on them.

Take advantage of the power of courageous journaling. It's the perfect midpoint between bottling things up inside and "exploding" on someone in a manner you'll later regret. Plus, it gives you time to pause and get clear on the issues in your tissues so you can take the most efficient actions to overcome them.

Remember, there's always a solution to most everything. There may be things to work out, but there's always a solution. Courageous journaling is a great way to discover YOUR solutions.

"*Writing about your thoughts and feelings helps clarify them. Whenever you write a sentence you simultaneously read the sentence, and when you read the sentence you are sparked to ponder the thought or feeling behind what you just wrote. So journaling creates a productive kind of dialogue with yourself.*"

—**Dennis Palumbo, M.A., MFT,**
Author and Psychotherapist

Chapter 4

Discover Your Power

I just love a good comeback story. Heck, I consider myself to be one—and I love sharing others. This chapter gets into rich detail about how to journal your own comeback story. If you're not in need of a great comeback yourself, you probably know someone who is.

We all do. So sharing what you learn from this chapter with someone you love could change their life forever and make you their hero!

Nearly all of us are close to someone whose life has been impacted by drug addiction or alcoholism. These are very serious medical conditions that require love, compassion, and intervention by family members and trained professionals.

However, what is often overlooked in therapeutic treatments for drug addiction and alcoholism is the healing power of journaling. As I've mentioned previously, journaling is the least expensive form of therapy I know, and it can play a HUGE role in overcoming addiction to drugs and alcohol.

This point is expressed beautifully in a blog post by Deb Earleywine, which she was gracious enough to share with our Create Write Now tribe. Deb is a valued and much-loved member of our community, and I am proud to share her blog post with you right here.

Journaling Puts You in the Driver's Seat

By Deb Earleywine

Nine years ago, I almost lost my life to alcoholism. I was in the Emergency Room and my heart almost stopped because the level of alcohol in my blood was sky high.

It wasn't the first time my parents had taken me to the ER in order to save my life. A worried doctor decided on the spot to send me immediately to a treatment center for alcoholics.

I'd been drinking for 20 years—I started when I was just fifteen. I drank throughout my teen years and into my twenties, but things really accelerated to an out-of-control type of drinking when I hit my thirties.

As a divorced, single mom with several bad relationships behind me, I got to the point where I just couldn't function without alcohol. It had to be the first thing I had in the morning and the last thing I had at night. I drank to celebrate good things and to drown out the bad. Alcohol was in every single aspect of my life and it became a vicious daily circle for me.

In 2004 I fell into an extremely toxic relationship with a guy, and things spun out of control.

He knew exactly how to push my buttons; he was controlling and very mentally cruel. In response, I would drink in order to cope and numb myself to the abuse I was undergoing. So, by 2007, I simply could NOT get through the day without a drink.

The referral to rehab was a turning point for me, the beginning of my journey to sobriety. I was fortunate to have a loving family to support me, and thankfully, while I was in rehab, I learned how to keep a journal as part of my therapy. It was my first experience of pouring out my feelings onto paper.

My first journal was about my toxic relationship. When I go back and read it now, I can see what I actually endured. I am so incredibly thankful I learned how to write my feelings out daily and date each and every entry.

My journal gave me a safe place to express all of my emotions—the anger, the frustration, the grief—and also me hope for a better life. It was a tool to help me plan a strategy to deal with my cravings. It became a daily regimen for me and I believe it can be a tool to help all people dealing with addiction.

I have stacks of journals and have continued my writing therapy since 2007. I truly believe it is one of the reasons that I just celebrated nine years of sobriety this past October!

Journaling lets you be the driver of your destiny. It is within you to put those thoughts and words, whether they are good or bad, onto paper and let out the emotions you may be dealing with at the moment. It is very empowering.

As you journal and then look back on those words on paper, maybe even many years down the road, it gives you strength and insight into the many twists and turns that life can throw at you. I am often amazed that something as simple as pen-to-paper therapy became such a key tool in my recovery.

Whatever your struggles, whether simple or complex, journaling is a chance to write YOUR story and get those feelings "out there." It has been a fantastic coping tool for me and it can be for you too! It will take you to places that you never dreamed were possible.

* * *

Deb Earleywine is a mom and spends her time caring for her family, including her father, who has dementia. She loves writing and communicating with people who struggle with addiction. She is an avid animal lover and enjoys painting.

> *"Journaling can be very helpful with addiction because it compels you to look at yourself honestly and with compassion and intent. This can be extremely valuable in the process of addiction recovery."*

—Dennis Palumbo, M.A., MFT, Author and Psychotherapist

Get It All Out!

Recovery from alcoholism or drug addiction is a huge struggle. There is no way to sugarcoat this fact. Journaling is an amazing tool that will help you put your days into perspective when something good or bad is going on in your life.

When you don't hold back and you journal all of your raw thoughts and emotions, you can then draw inner strength from what you've poured onto paper. This truth is even more powerful in darker moments when you are tempted to drink or turn to any addictive behavior.

In moments of despair, pouring your feelings onto paper puts them right in front of you to read, which means you're literally looking at them. It's almost as if you're watching yourself in a mirror. By putting yourself in this role of a self-observer, you have a better chance of stopping yourself from taking an action you might later regret.

Nearly everyone I speak with who has been involved in a drug or alcohol recovery program agrees that journaling is a tremendous coping tool that should be emphasized much more in rehabilitation programs and facilities.

Why? Because by journaling you get everything out. The good, the bad, and the ugly. It forces you to look at what you're feeling and come face to face with it. Journaling leaves you with no place to hide. When you grab a pen and pour your guts out onto paper, you have no option but to get real about the issues in your tissues.

When you are completely authentic and honest about what you share in your journal, you will gain greater clarity of thought in return. You will also receive strong messages about actions you should or shouldn't take.

If you struggle with addiction, journaling will help you set your compass so you can get your life moving in the right direction. Even if it's just the right direction for TODAY!

If you're struggling with addiction or alcoholism, the dreams and goals you write about this morning could just be the dreams and goals you have for TODAY. When you put pen to paper and write down what your feelings, dreams, and goals are just for today, they will become hardwired into your brain.

Going through this exercise in the morning could be what gives you the strength to make it through days when you feel like you might reach for a drink or turn to another addictive behavior.

Deb Earleywine tells me that when recovering alcoholics want to drink, they may be tempted to drink because they are down about something. However, they may also want to drink to celebrate an accomplishment. When Deb finds herself in these moments, she is able to pour what she's feeling onto paper and face it head-on at that moment, which gives her the strength not to drink.

Look Back and Learn

Deb Earleywine also says she draws tremendous strength throughout her recovery by being able to flip back through her journal and read about bad days when she was tempted to drink, so she can see how she got through that day without drinking.

For example, if she's having a day when she's tempted to drink, she'll journal about her feelings and face them head-on. In addition, she will look back at her previous journal entries to see how she got through other days when she was tempted to drink. She says by being able to read about how she made it through those moments, she draws the strength she needs to get through the moment at hand.

This is a very powerful practice that you or a loved one can mimic if you're in recovery and dealing with addiction on a day-to-day basis.

Through journaling, you can always look back and see what you did to get through a rough patch, and you can say, "Hey, I got through it and I made it. It was rough and I got through it, and here's how I did it. And there's no reason why I can't do it again."

When you read your past journal entries you can see how many trials and tribulations you went through and how you overcame them. This will pump you up with pride, which will help keep you strong and moving on a good path in life. And as I've said before, it beats the hell out of paying a therapist.

Or as Deb Earleywine proudly reports, "Journaling has been the only therapeutic type of tool that has really, really helped me. And it doesn't cost me $200 an hour."

Be a Gift to Others

The best things in life are free, and I repeat the point many times in this book that journaling is a wonderful form of no-cost therapy. However, it can also be a gift you share with other people.

If you are in recovery from alcoholism or drug addiction, I am certain the insights you've learned in this chapter will help you. However, you can also be a gift to others in recovery by sharing these insights with them.

I made a point earlier in this chapter that journaling is underemphasized, or not even mentioned, in most recovery programs. If you're in recovery or know someone struggling with addiction, you can be a shining light by turning them on to the therapeutic benefits of journaling that you're learning about in this book.

Taking this simple step will give you a wonderful feeling inside you can carry with you every day—and who knows how many lives you may change for the better.

The Lesson In All This

Deb Earleywine likes to say that you can accomplish anything in life you put your mind to through journaling, including sobriety. She also says that journaling is the most powerful tool she's used to keep herself on a good path.

The lesson here is very simple and straightforward: YOU can do the same!

When you're real and honest with yourself, and you pour your true thoughts and feelings into your journal, they become more real and personal. The internal messages and guidance you receive when you're sincere and authentic with your journaling also become more etched in your consciousness.

Expressive writing is your no-cost therapist and your best friend. If you're in recovery, your journal is the person you can always turn to. You can talk to your journal anytime you want like it's a best friend you can trust more than anyone.

Deb Earleywine believes that journaling is her personal counselor, accountability partner, and number-one advocate. I agree with her completely.

If you or someone you love suffers from alcoholism or addiction, I encourage you to tap into the extraordinary healing power of journaling.

Your Journaling Prompt

Facing the challenges that come with alcohol or drug recovery can be complicated, so it's a good idea to keep your journaling prompt simple. The first thing you can do is to just get started. Grab a pen and a pad and just start writing. Be real, be raw, and be honest. The key is to JUST DO IT.

Deb Earleywine suggests that a great first step is to set a basic goal. Your goal could be to not drink that day, or that week, or in the next 10 minutes. Write about your goal as if you are talking it through with your own personal therapist or friend.

Just be free and let it loose. Don't hold anything back. You'll be amazed at what comes back to you through your intuition or inner voice.

You just have to start. You just have to give this amazing tool a shot and start writing. This simple step can be what it takes to get you, or someone you know, in recovery, heading down a healthy path.

Be good to yourself and make things easy and uncomplicated. As you begin your journaling practice, open up and reveal yourself and everything you're feeling for just five or 10 minutes. Start small and build it up as you go. Move forward in incremental steps that feel good to you. This is the key.

Starting with small steps can help you achieve BIG goals. You just have to commit and GO FOR IT!

"Writing about stressful events, whether it's pain or addiction, helps you get out of your head and into an 'observer role' through which you can look at your life from a more objective point of view. As it relates to addiction, this is especially helpful when you read past journal entries as an observer and are able to see themes, habits, and feelings that pop up continually. This can help you catch yourself before you turn to an addictive substance like food, drugs, or alcohol to deal with physical or emotional pain."

—Dr. Joe Tatta, DPT, CNS

Chapter 5

Express Your Emotions

Have you noticed that many men tend to keep their feelings bottled up inside because they've been taught to be tough and not show their emotions? It's true.

Now, I know I'm not supposed to make generalized statements like this about the sexes anymore. But who cares, I'm going to do it anyway. Because let's face it, men and women are different, whether it's politically correct to admit it or not.

Here's another direct statement about the sexes: not enough men journal! There are several reasons for this. As I stated a moment ago, many men have been conditioned by society to bottle up their feelings and present a "strong" front to the world, even when they're aching inside.

Also, many men associate journaling with "keeping a diary," which doesn't sound like a very masculine thing to do. In addition, many men have been taught to believe that only little girls and women keep diaries. Men, on the other hand, are expected to release their emotions by chopping wood, yelling, or punching something.

I intend to change this mindset and get more guys into journaling to deal with the issues in their tissues.

Now, ladies, if it sounds like this chapter is going to be slanted toward the men...it's because it is. However, that doesn't mean you should jump forward to the next chapter! After all, you probably have men in your life who could use a healthy outlet for expressing their feelings and dealing with their issues.

What you'll learn by reading the next several pages will help you understand more about what makes men tick, and you'll gain the insight you need to steer the man or men in your life toward expressive journaling. And some of the benefits of journaling I explore in this chapter apply equally to men *and* women.

Plus, you're going to learn about an amazing young man named Ollie Aplin, who is a valued Create Write Now tribe member, and founder of the website *www.mindjournals.com*. This magnificent website is dedicated to teaching men how to increase their satisfaction and energize their lives through the numerous benefits of expressive journaling.

Ollie has an incredible story to share, which you'll learn more about in just a minute. However, I can tell you that during his young life, Ollie has dealt with a lot of anxiety, and he tells me that journaling is a way for him to calm his thought process.

Like a lot of men, he says his mind operates in a way that is similar to flipping between TV channels that have different "programs" running on them. Ollies says that when he's anxious or under stress, his brain seems to fire off in different directions...bouncing among different "channels" in rapid fashion.

Fortunately, Ollie discovered that journaling is a way to calm his mind and tackle issues in a holistic and complete way without jumping from one mental channel to the next while never fully dealing with his issues.

In addition, Ollie says that he enjoys going back and reading past journal entries because it is very grounding and it has a magical way of depressurizing his brain.

I could tell you more, but instead I'd prefer to share Ollie's story through a wonderful blog post he wrote for CreateWriteNow.com, which I am republishing here.

Why I Started Journaling

By Ollie Aplin

How many times have you gone to write something, and just not known where to start? There are so many places to start, it's hard to just pick one word or thought. And as you stare longer and longer at the blank page, the more crippled you feel—and the words in your mind seem to disappear.

This is not writer's block. It's that our busy minds are too noisy to find focus. And as an anxiety sufferer, this is exactly how I've felt for years when I've tried to keep a journal.

Journaling was prescribed to me back in 2008 after I suffered a mental breakdown. I'd lost my mum to suicide two years before that and had never dealt with my chaotic childhood of living with a bipolar mum.

Instead, from the age of five, I was told by mum to never tell anyone what was going on at home. Especially my dad. They were no longer together and Mum wanted to keep her life private from everyone. But the promise I made had a deep and long-lasting effect on me. Not talking meant not expressing how I felt. And as I got older and Mum's condition stayed undiagnosed and got more erratic—I locked up my emotions even further, eventually becoming emotionally numb to everything.

So in my mid-teens, I turned to drugs and alcohol. I was pretty much stoned throughout all of secondary school. And by the age of 18, I overdosed one night after partying too hard following a suicide attempt by Mum. After several more attempts, she finally succeeded in ending her life in November 2005, when I was 19.

It took me until April 2008 to finally seek help. By then I was utterly broken. No longer functioning as a human being—I could barely eat, sleep or talk.

But when I did eventually make it into therapy and I sat there in the counsellor's chair, I didn't really know what to say. I'd not spoken to anyone about the things that had been happening for all those years with Mum.

Because she told me not to. And just because she was dead didn't make any difference. Mum was a terrifying person. Don't get me wrong, she was incredible and the most loving mum you could ever imagine. But the bipolar side to her was this extremely intense, paranoid and sad person that had no relation to who she really was.

Not knowing how she would be from one day to the next meant you lived in fear of this alternative side of her being unleashed.

So sitting there in therapy and being asked to talk was one of the most uncomfortable things I'd experienced. It felt disloyal and I was paranoid that Mum would find out. So I skirted about the issues, gave top level facts about the suicide attempts but sat there waiting for my therapist to fix me.

Turns out that's not how therapy works. It requires talking—a key part that was far from normal for me.

With this in mind, my therapist prescribed journaling and it literally changed my entire life. Nine years on and I'm still going strong, with my journal by my side through all the things that life throws at me.

But I've never found it easy. Finding the time, the words and the feelings is a huge barrier for me even now.

The amazing thing about counseling is that it's a lot like having a personal trainer at the gym. They provide the workout, you just have to do the work. They lead the session and keep pushing you to say more, do more, try harder. You just have to be there and provide the effort.

With a journal though, it's just you and the page. You have to do all the work yourself.

So after researching and trying to find a journal that would help me to write—and not being able to find one, I knew it was something I had to create. Being a designer helped but knowing what I wanted from a guided journal helped even more.

After six months of designing and testing, my girlfriend and I launched MindJournal on Kickstarter in February 2016— the world's first guided journal just for men. And it blew up.

Now, over a year later, MindJournal has helped thousands of guys from all over the world kickstart their journaling habit. And the reason it works so well is that every time you go to write, you always have something to say.

MindJournal has been designed with a carefully created writing program.

The program is compiled of 30 exercises that start off relatively easy and get tougher and tougher the more you work through the journal. Every exercise also provides you with an opportunity to check in with how you're feeling and there's motivation from me every step of the way.

The reason it's such a powerful tool is because it works. Us guys rarely like to talk about our feelings or what's on our minds. And that's OK, as long as you're still looking after yourself. MindJournal is there when guys either don't want to talk or are unable to do so—providing them with a space to privately look after themselves.

* * *

Ollie Aplin *and is the creator of MindJournal. You can find out more about his movement at* www.mindjournals.com.

Slow Down and Connect

One reason you should journal, as a man, is because it forces you to slow down in a world where you feel rushed constantly. Journaling is about taking the pace of your life down a notch or two and being more mindful and present.

This helps you connect emotionally with what's going on around you and within you. If you fail to do this, you may not realize how your work is making you feel, or how your friends are making you feel, or how your partner is making you feel.

Journaling allows you to slow down and get in touch with these issues. It's a way to get them off of your shoulders and onto paper, which can really lighten your load.

These days it is so easy to rush through the day without touching base with how you really feel about anything. Many men believe that if you avoid an issue it will just go away. But this isn't how it works. When you avoid thinking of an issue instead of dealing with it, your avoidance only serves to shove the issue deeper and deeper inside you.

Put Your Issues in Front of Your Face

Journaling is the ideal way to unbury your issues by putting them down on paper right in front of your nose where you can't miss them. Writing about the issues in your tissues compels you to pause and think about how the different aspects, or compartments, of your life make you feel. It gives you time to gather your thoughts and relax. It also helps you separate facts from feelings.

Here's what I mean. Rather than just write down the facts about what you did during the day, write down the emotions you FEEL that are related to what you did. This frees you up to be more emotional and fully human.

A lot of men struggle with this. Are you one of them? Do you have a problem accessing your more vulnerable side? If you do, today is the day you can overcome this.

Remember, nobody is going to read your journal except you. So you don't have to worry what your buddies will think. Journaling gives you a safe outlet where you can be comfortable being vulnerable and emotional without the worry of being seen by other "dudes" as week or unmanly.

Hang Out in Your Own Mental Man Cave

Think of your journaling practice as your own mental man cave! A place where you can go and just be YOU. A place where you don't have to worry about anyone telling you that you are right or wrong for the way you feel.

Journaling also gives you a great way to say anything you want about someone else. If you need to blow off some steam without making a fool of yourself, your journal is the perfect place.

Your journal is also the perfect place to work out your feelings or have a dialogue with someone before you speak to them in person. Before you say something mean or hot-headed to someone impulsively that you might regret, you can cuss a blue streak in your journal instead.

By working through what you'd like to say to someone in your journal, you'll have a much more authentic and well-thought-out conversation with them when you actually speak.

Think about it. How many times have you thought about things you wish you would have said a day or two after you've had a conversation with someone. We've all gone through this experience, and it's frustrating.

If you use your journal to work through conversations BEFORE you talk to someone, you'll never experience this frustration again.

Also, when you pour your heart and your true feelings into your journal, the Universe tends to fill your intuition with answers, lessons, and guidance. This is one of the great surprises for men when they begin a journaling practice!

Tap into What's Already Inside You

Many men are pleasantly surprised when they discover how much louder their inner voice becomes when they allow themselves to open up and express their feelings through journaling. The same thing will happen to you.

That gut instinct you've always kind of trusted will become a loud, confident voice of certainty you can depend on seven days a week, 365 days a year!

What you'll discover is that you don't need to read 15,000 blog posts and go to 26 seminars and watch 15 hours of YouTube videos to learn about YOU. You won't need to do that because everything you're looking for is already inside you.

You just need to tap into it, listen to it, and trust it! Journaling helps you access and unlock what's already inside you. And what you unlock can be amazing and really surprise you.

In fact, what you'll discover through journaling is that within you is a treasure chest of answers and solutions. As I've said, journaling is the cheapest form of therapy. And what guy doesn't like to save money!

When you put your feelings on paper, it's amazing how certainty and clarity of thought come racing back at you. And none of your friends have to know you have your own private therapist!

Bust Free from Being a Hunter

Like a lot of guys, you may have been conditioned by society to believe you have to always be on the hunt. You have to hunt down lovers and mates, hunt down a better car, hunt down a higher-paying job, and hunt down a bigger house.

Journaling frees you from this grind because through expressive writing you no longer have to chase and hunt down answers to life's important questions. Instead, you can get quiet and reflective with your journal, and let the answers flow freely to you.

You can let "things" catch up with you, instead of expending all your energy trying to chase things down.

As a man, it can be liberating to learn that not everything has to be an arduous hunt. When you journal, you are free to allow calmness, quiet, and reflection into your life. Journaling gives you permission to slow down and let things show up at your mental doorstep.

Remember, what you've been hunting for may be trying like hell to catch up with you. So sit still for a minute, grab your pen and paper, and allow this to happen.

The Lesson in All This

For the lesson in all this I turned to my good friend, Ollie Aplin, who interacts every day with men who journal. If you're like most of the men Ollie engages with, you'll find that journaling will help you become more productive and focused.

Ollie tells me he's achieved far more than he could imagine by simply stopping and writing down all the thoughts, feelings, and ideas that were "bouncing around his head." (*His words!*)

Do the same, and you'll be amazed at what pops off the page and impacts you. You'll have light-bulb moments and feel a lot of clarity. You'll discover answers that you never knew were hiding inside you.

What you use to drain your energy hunting for will now flow to you with ease and grace.

Over time, you'll be able to look back and see things you would not have accomplished if you had not gone through the journaling process to confront the issues in your tissues.

Stick with your journaling routine and you'll find that your "man cave" reflection time will empower you to be more focused and energized. By bringing your feelings and emotions forward, you'll feel less like a hamster on a wheel who is moving frantically through the day without really feeling anything at all.

Remember, action doesn't always equal productivity if your actions lack purpose and direction. When you journal and allow yourself to tap into your intuition and gain clarity about what's really important to you, your actions will be more precise and exact, and you'll experience greater productivity in your life.

Come on guys, you CAN do this!

Your Journaling Prompt

Your journaling prompt for his chapter comes in two parts, and it comes to you from Ollie Aplin.

Part One – Just Start Writing

If you're a man and you haven't journaled, here's a great way to get started. Grab a pen and pad and at the end of each day write down what you did that day. If you prefer to write in the morning like many journalers, you can simply write about what you did the day before.

However, after a couple weeks, move beyond merely writing about what you did. Dig a little deeper and begin to write about how you FEEL about what you did. If what you did made you happy, sad, or angry...write about it!

As the weeks go by, continue to dig a little deeper into your feelings so nothing is left bottled up inside you. As I said previously, when you begin to put your feelings down on paper, answers and solutions to the challenges you face will begin to flow to you through your intuition.

Again, this will eliminate the need to "hunt" down solutions to your problems or answers to your questions. Instead, they will just come to you and you will feel them with certainty.

Part Two – Empty Your Stress Bucket

As you feel more confident and established in your journaling routine, take things up a notch by doing the "stress bucket" exercise. I want to thank Ollie Aplin for sharing it with me, along with the visual images that go with it (*You'll be seeing them in just a minute*).

The stress-bucket exercise is a great journaling technique and it can be a lot of fun. All you have to do is draw a simple bucket and fill it with the stressful "stuff" that happened to you during the day. When you do this, you'll have a strong visual representation of how much stress you have in your life.

And for the love of Pete, don't worry about how well you draw. A stick-figure bucket will do just fine. Just draw it and fill it with the things that are stressing you out.

Drawing your stress bucket is also a nice way to get past any intimidation you may feel about having a blank piece of paper in front of you if you're not sure where to start or what to write.

This exercise is not only a great way to write about what's stressing you, but also a great way to step aside with some objectivity and SEE what's stressing you.

If you see that your stress bucket is full, then you know you need to take actions that will empower you to empty it...or at least make it less full... so you can reduce the amount of tension in your life.

Plus, when you draw your stress bucket you don't have to follow a rigid set of rules. Remember, you'll be in your mental man cave when you're doing this. You can draw your bucket any way you want because YOU are in charge. This gives you a tremendous feeling of control and confidence.

The following three pages include visual illustrations of the stress-bucket exercise that show you step by step how to incorporate this simple but powerful technique into your journaling practice.

I want to send a big shout-out and thank you to my good friend Ollie Aplin, who provided these illustrations.

ENTRY SIXTEEN
STRESS BUCKET

When there's loads of stuff doing your head in, it's sometimes hard to know what's causing you to feel so stressed out.

You can only tackle your stress when you know exactly what is stressing you out.

So how do you locate the sources of your stress? Simple, draw your Stress Bucket. The Stress Bucket is a tool created by leading psychologists, Alison Brabban and Douglas Turkington. And it's hugely effective at nailing what's really stressing you out, and how the way you're dealing with it is having an effect on you.

Everyone has a different size bucket, depending on how much stress they can carry. Yours might be small or it could be huge. Either way buckets contain water and water equals stress. And how many things are stressing you out determines how full your bucket it is.

The Stress Bucket has a little tap at the bottom though, like a keg of beer. Every time you look after yourself and do something that relieves your stress, water is let out of it. The less you look after yourself, the less the tap opens. And the fuller the bucket gets.

Use the Stress Bucket diagram on the next page to find all the things that are causing you to feel stressed. Draw a water line on the bucket to mark where your current stress level is. And at the bottom where the little tap is, write down all the things that you do to look after yourself and help relieve your stress.

DATE:

DAILY CHECK-IN

HOW DO YOU FEEL TODAY?

positive	safe	grateful	relieved
happy	bored	unhappy	scared
hopeful	tired	frustrated	trapped
stressed	hurt	furious	alive
nervous	eager	calm	worthless
tense	angry	strong	guilty
anxious	excited	neutral	bitter
determined	irritated	regretful	shocked
glad	disappointed	lonely	sad
worried	content	low	energetic
insecure	negative	confident	unsure
confused	annoyed	restless	
proud	inspired	surprised	

TODAY'S INTENTIONS / ACHIEVEMENTS:

1.
2.
3.

3 THINGS YOU'RE GRATEFUL FOR TODAY:

1.
2.
3.

YOUR HAPPY HOUR FOR TODAY:

DATE

HURDLES

ENTRY 16 / 30

THE STRESS BUCKET

In the bucket, list everything that's making you feel stressed. Then, where the tap is at the bottom, list all the things that help relieve your stress.

M

You can only tackle stress when you
know what is stressing you out

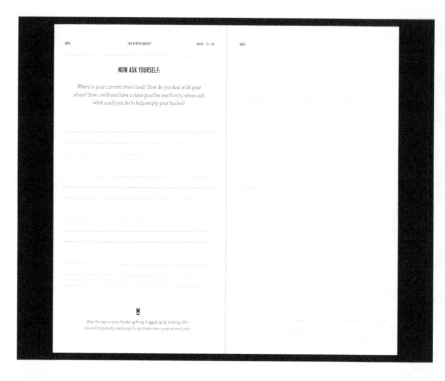

Once again, I'd like to thank Ollie Aplin for providing these illustrations. You can learn more about Ollie and his incredible journaling programs for men at www.mindjournals.com.

Now, start drawing your bucket!

> *"One of the benefits of journaling is you're getting your true feelings out. When you keep things bottled up, you become like a pressure cooker and eventually things will explode. Journaling relieves this pressure, which is very healthy for you."*
>
> —**Jenetta Haim**, Founder of Stressfree Management®;
> Lifestyle and Health Management Expert

Chapter 6

Rekindle the Light in Your Life

Sometimes in life you may slowly become aware that you are *here* and realize that you'd rather be *there*—wherever *there* may be. Or, to put it another way, it is not unusual to discover the day-to-day life you are leading is far removed from the life you once envisioned for yourself.

In fact, the distance between your current life and the life you envisioned may in your mind look and feel like an enormous chasm.

So how do you bridge this chasm and go from where you are in life to where you want to be? One way you can do this is by writing a new story about your life, which is a journaling technique I'm going to cover in great detail in upcoming chapters.

However, this approach to journaling may not be easy for you, or it may be a practice you need to work up to slowly. Or perhaps you may feel that before you can write a new life story you need to rekindle the light in the life you're currently living.

This is exactly how Create Write Now tribe member Anthony Billoni felt about his life about a dozen years ago. Put simply, Anthony was "stuck in a rut." He had a wife and two children and he was doing what it took to take care of them. But something inside told him he could be doing more to live a passionate life in which he truly made the most of his gifts.

Through journaling, Anthony began to cross the chasm from where he was to where he wanted to be. They say every journey begins with the first step. For Anthony, the spark that got his feet moving was his own unique approach to journaling.

Anthony's *journaling journey* is best detailed through a blog post he wrote and shared with the Create Write Now tribe. It is published on CreateWriteNow.com, and I am happy to republish it here.

My Journaling Journey

By Anthony Billoni

Maybe turning 50 was a flashing yellow light. Maybe I was afraid the light was about to turn red—on reaching significant goals I had set for myself.

What came to be my daily journaling habit was years in the making. Recently I came across an online journal from close to 10 years ago. Just one entry.

Before getting married, I took myself out of the booze-soaked 4am nightclub business in 1992. While trying to find the sweet spot of leveraging my crowd-building skill in the real world I found the Creative Problem Solving Institute (CPSI) (cpsiconference.org). Here I found people that thought like the creatives in my clubs but were bringing cool ideas and energies into business. I produced CPSI's events and ran with it until 9/11 happened and all conferences took a hit. I was back to searching. Getting married and raising two beautiful daughters found me drifting away from the passion of creating. I was gaining weight and eating poorly. I was just making a paycheck happen and keeping my family moving forward.

Around 2008–09 events I can't remember made the blinking yellow light glow brighter and I began to inch into eating better and doing home-grown fitness activities. One day a friend asked me if I wanted to join him in going through *The Artist's Way* by Julia Cameron. The lessons and the deep uncoverings of what was leading me "away from the page," as Cameron puts it, resonated and I worked my way through all 12 lessons. One "must have," in order to keep the lessons going, was the daily Morning Pages (MP). The instruction was: fill three pages first thing in the morning each day. It functioned as a brain dump. A sort of Zen emptying of the vessel so I had room to fill it with free flowing creative energy and turn outward for all the world to see.

I went in with the intent to get back to my creative writing. Now more than seven years later I came away with so much more. Do I write every day? Almost. Do I do it first thing in the morning? Maybe 50% of the time. What began as "Get what was in my head out" led to writing about all kinds of stuff. So much else pushed to the surface. Doubts, fears, confusions, upsets and joy. So I now journal to get to the leading edge of my clearly defined passion. Along the way the MP led me to focus enough on completing my first 5,000 word short story with another in the works. I also completed about two dozen blog posts and started a newsletter to get them out. Most important, I have transformed my passion to help people grow through creativity into a consulting practice.

I started the MP full of fear that I was about to lose the path to my passion forever. Today, I eagerly ask, "Where to next?" To those reading this, I say whether you have a definite aim and clear motivation for your journal and reflection experience, or whether you have a wish that something will happen, or maybe you just want more clarity—get to the page! Doing it each day cleared the path for me to only focus—and stay focused—on what was important.

* * *

Anthony Billoni has distinguished himself as a career coach and leadership expert at abcre8.com. Additionally, he creates results-oriented capacity-building, marketing, and advocacy programs for Tobacco-Free Western New York at Roswell Park Cancer Institute. Over the past 30 years, he has done the same for the Creative Education Foundation, Art On Wheels, Burchfield-Penney Art Center, The Park School of Buffalo, and Young Audiences of WNY.

His passion is community-building, the arts, wellness, cultural heritage, and volunteering. He is a faculty member of the Creative Problem Solving Institute and holds a master's degree in Creativity and Change Leadership from Buffalo State College. As a founding member and past President of the Buffalo Niagara Medical Campus Rotary Club, he values service above self.

Clear Away Gaps and Barriers

One of my favorite lines from Anthony's blog post is: *What began as "Get what was in my head out" led to writing about all kinds of stuff.*

This is a very raw approach to beginning YOUR journaling journey, and it can be this simple. The key is to just start writing with reckless abandon without regard to style or structure. Just let it loose and go for it. When you do this you'll quickly begin to write about the issues in your tissues. We all have issues, and this direct approach to journaling is a great way to confront them head-on!

This unapologetic method of writing is a great way to recognize and clear up a lot of hidden barriers in your life. Things you may have long ago buried beneath the surface will bubble up right before your eyes as you let your honest feelings pour forth.

It is often these hidden barriers that are keeping you from living the life you envisioned for yourself. If the vision you once saw for yourself seems to be so far off in the distance you can no longer see it, this raw form of journaling may be the spark that rekindles the light in your life.

Empty Your Brain and Watch What Happens!

The key to getting started is to write with no agenda of any kind. Just empty your brain and clear the decks. Don't worry about being clean, neat, or formal. Just put your foot on the gas pedal and go. Your writing may feel rough and jagged around the edges, but who cares. Just do it anyway!

Remember, no one's going to grade your journal. So just let loose and have at it!

When you just let go and allow your unedited thoughts and feelings to pour forth, a funny thing will happen. Over time, your writing will evolve from "I did this, and I did that" to "This is how what I've done has made me feel, and this is what I'm going to DO about it."

As you get the issues in your tissues out in the open, you will feel yourself being fueled with action plans that will help you break down barriers and old belief systems.

When this happens, you'll feel motivated to write about what you want to achieve, and then your intuition will further fuel you with ideas about actions you can take to make things happen in your life.

Next thing you know, the chasm that separates you from where you are and where you want to be will look like much less of a chasm, and more like a gap you know with certainty you can cross.

Be Very Honest with Yourself

The key to getting results from this form of journaling is to be very honest with yourself. Don't hold anything back. Again, nobody is going to read your journal but YOU. So if you have issues in your tissues (and we all do), spill your guts and put them down on paper.

As you do this, accept that you may not have immediate answers to questions about your issues. But if you make an open and honest effort to get them down on paper, the answers you seek will flow your way faster than you think.

As a result of this journaling style, Anthony Billoni tells me he doesn't carry around "should have," "could have," or "wish I'd done that differently" thoughts in his head for more than a day or so. This is because he has learned to cleanse and release these thoughts through his journaling.

When you put your true feelings down on paper, you'll avoid having longstanding drama in your life because you'll be able to confront your issues head-on.

For example, if you have a disagreement with someone, it is perfectly normal to later think, "I wish I had said this," or, "I wish I had said that." When you write down what you wish you had said in your journal, you may find it's very easy to then pick up the phone and have a direct conversation during which you express how you REALLY feel.

This is an ideal way to use your journal if you tend to bottle your feelings up inside and are slow to express what's really on your mind. Bottling up your emotions can be quite stressful on your body. And stress is one of the leading causes of illness, especially heart disease.

At a minimum, this is a great form of journaling to let go of pent-up emotions by transferring them from your head to a pad of paper.

This alone will lighten your load so you can rekindle the light in your life!

Don't Worry About the Meaning of Life Just Yet

When you journal to rekindle the light in your life, another rule of thumb to follow is to keep things simple. In other words, don't feel the need to bend your brain trying to figure out the meaning of life or why you were put on Earth.

Is there a place in your journaling journey to contemplate these issues? Absolutely. But I recommend working your way up to this more emotionally complex form of journaling.

It's perfectly fine to start simple and just write about the day-to-day issues in your tissues that revolve around how you feel about your work, or how well you're getting along with a co-worker, or a friend, or your significant other.

Also, when you keep things simple, it becomes easier for you to slowly realize through your writing what is truly important to you. For example, as you cleanse and release issues you may create room in your mind to begin writing your own personal vision statement.

Anthony Billoni tells me that through this form of journaling he gradually developed a straightforward personal vision that states: "I profit from bringing freedom and creativity to people and organizations. And I know that the word *profit* doesn't always mean money."

What you'll find when you journal to rekindle the light in your life is that you no longer carry around worry and doubt. That's because your writing will help you release these feelings, which clears space for you to instead create newfound feelings of clarity and certainty.

Put an End to Overwhelm

Another benefit of journaling to rekindle the light in your life is that you'll gain the ability to minimize or eliminate what is overwhelming in your life. Nearly everyone I speak to these days complains about being overwhelmed by technology, an ever-expanding to-do list, email, and expectations being placed on them by others.

"I just can't keep up with it all" is a common cry for help you hear from friends, family, and business colleagues.

However, most of the time, you CHOOSE to ALLOW yourself to become overwhelmed to the point that you can even become addicted to it. But life doesn't have to be this way. In fact, escaping being overwhelmed and living at a more manageable pace would definitely be a great way to rekindle your life.

So grab your pen and pad and do a free-flowing brain dump in which you write down exactly what's creating your never-ending state of being overwhelmed. As you do, consider asking yourself these types of questions.

- Am I checking email too often?
- Am I overcommitting to others?
- Have I become addicted to Facebook?
- Do I watch way too much news on TV, and get upset about it?

Write down in detail what is causing you to feel as if you have no time to breathe, or no time to just be YOU. Next, ask your journal what you can do to cut back and declutter your brain. Using the previous list as an example, the answers that come shooting back to you through your intuition may look like this:

- Check my email just three times a day (*people can wait for your response*)
- Only make commitments that fit in my schedule comfortably (*you're allowed to say "no"*)
- Don't spend over 20 minutes a day surfing Facebook (*you lived a lot of years without it*)
- READ the news on my favorite website 20 minutes each day and tune out the madness that floods TV news each night (*you'll stay fully informed on what actually impacts your life*)

Just because technology has made it possible for a constant stream of information (most of which is negative) to firehose you 24/7 doesn't mean you have to allow yourself to be pummeled by it.

Casey Demchak, who is featured in Chapter 8, lives by a simple slogan that helps him control the impact modern technology has in his life: "New-School Tools. But At an Old-School Pace."

Casey tells me he 1) checks his email three times a day; 2) reads the news for 15 to 20 minutes on his favorite news website; 3) and spends no more than 30 minutes a day on social media. Yet his business thrives and he feels fully informed about what's going on in the world.

From what I can tell, the only thing he's missing out on by living this way is a lot of needless, mind-bending drama and stress!

When you take the time to list the things in your journal that are creating a feeling of being overwhelm in your life, you will be able to look at the list and realize how simple it can be to eliminate most of that which is causing you to feel overwhelmed.

You'll understand that overwhelm is a choice, not a condition that sneaks up and attaches itself to your brain. When you know this, you'll feel empowered to eliminate it from your life.

And when an overwhelm addict tries to drain your energy and overload your mind or your schedule, you'll have all the confidence you need to simply say, "No. I'm maxed out and I have as much on my plate as I can handle comfortably right now."

Think about it: all the technology you have at your fingertips should make it easier for you to be more productive, so you have more time to be YOU.

So why does it seem to have the opposite effect on most people?

Get real with this topic in your journal. If you do, you'll be able to snuff out overwhelm, which is essential to rekindling the light in your life! Journaling to eliminate overwhelm is a fascinating and important topic that you'll learn even more about in Chapter 10.

The Lesson in All This

To quote Anthony Billoni, this unapologetic style of journaling "dispels the notion that journaling has to be a soft navel-gazing introspective exercise."

In fact, journaling has been a "power tool" for some of the most successful people in history. Why? Because it's honest, it's straightforward, and it forces you to open up and get real with yourself.

Also, this blunt form of journaling to rekindle the light in your life is popular among men, because it debunks the myth that journaling has to be over-emotional, mushy, and flowery. Instead, it can be edgy, direct, and hard-hitting.

But again, the key is to be honest with yourself!

If you're honest, journaling to reignite your life will help you find answers to all the concerns and questions you have about yourself. But you have to get down to the nitty-gritty, and you have to make journaling a habit.

When you write about the issues in your tissues, you can't just tell yourself happy bullshit stories. You have to be honest and dig into the details. You've heard the expression "Dance like no one is watching." Well, now it's time to internalize this expression: "Write like no one will ever read your journal but you."

This may not be easy at first. But it gets easier when you understand that the more honest your writing is, the greater the clarity is when the answers you seek come shooting back to you.

So do you want to rekindle the light in your life through journaling? Here's how you can get started.

Your Journaling Prompt

Journaling to rekindle the light in your life can be very powerful and getting started can be very simple. Your initial prompt is to grab a pen and start writing on a pad or notebook. And again, be very honest with yourself.

Anthony Billoni suggests that a great way to begin is to start with "what's on top." This means you can create some momentum in your daily routine by writing about what's going on in your life today.

When you get comfortable writing about the events of your day, you'll find that over time it's easier to stretch out and start looking at what's "under the hood," or examining what's really going on in your life.

For example, you may choose to journal about what you wish you would have said to someone during a important conversation. What you'll find is that by putting your honest thoughts down on paper you may gain the strength and courage to actually say it to them. Do this, and any tension you had built up about this conversation will be released.

So your primary prompt is to start with what's inside YOU and work your way out from there. Again, the key is to be completely HONEST about what's going on inside you.

To take it a step further, start writing about challenges you see coming your way. This gives you an opportunity to proactively work through a challenge before it takes you by surprise. If you can anticipate a challenge, write about how it makes you feel and how you'd like to react to it. Consider in your journal actions you can take, or conversation points you can make to deal with this challenge most effectively.

If you take these steps before the challenge actually lands on your plate, you'll be in a much stronger position when it does.

If you practice this open and authentic form of journaling day after day, week after week, and month after month, you'll find that you are able to operate from a much more commanding position, and this has everything to do with being able to rekindle the light in your life.

> *"In a world where we often wear "masks" as we play different roles in life, journaling alone in a room is often the only chance you have to be you, and to let your true thoughts and feelings pour forth onto paper. It's your chance to be honest with yourself and record exactly how you feel about anything. This brings about a great deal of personal empowerment."*

—**Jenetta Haim**, Founder of Stressfree Management®;
Lifestyle and Health Management Expert

Chapter 7

Create a New Life Story

I am proud to have Alison Laverty as part of my Create Write Now tribe because she is a truly wonderful person, and she has a very interesting story to share. Alison was raised in a violent, abusive background, and she turned to journaling as a teenager to express herself and her feelings.

What amazes me is that as a young woman living a very tough life, she intuitively turned to journaling as a means of healing herself and transforming her life. It took nearly two decades for her to feel as though she had healed, but through this time she stuck with her self-taught journaling practice.

Over time, Alison's life began to change and her journaling practice became more about writing her intentions for her future. This form of journaling motivated her to get focused and take action, so she could move from where she was to where she wanted to go.

Her actions began after she wrote her intentions. What Alison has discovered over time was that all of the intentions she wrote about 20 or more years ago have actually come true in ways she would have never imagined.

She literally used journaling to create a new life she had dreamed about. This is further proof that journaling not only helps you heal, but also helps you find the essence of your true self, and who you are being in the world. This gives you the foundation to move forward so you can identify your true purpose.

When you write the story of what you want your life to be, your intuition will literally speak to you and fuel you with actions you need to take. All you need to know is the *what* and the *why* of what you want.

The path toward what you desire will reveal itself a few stepping stones at a time, but over time the *how* and *when* aspect of what you manifest will take shape in ways you never would have expected.

Bottom line: it's useful to write good stories because there's magic in them.

Alison Laverty shared a wonderful blog post on CreateWriteNow. com that provides an eye-opening illustration of how telling better stories through journaling healed and transformed her life. I invite you to enjoy it here.

What Stories Do You Tell Yourself?

By Alison Laverty

How do you maintain a connection to yourself and cut out the noise around you?

It is not easy to decipher where the noise comes from because every day we tell stories to ourselves. We blame others and the world around us for making our life miserable, yet it is we who really make up these stories in our mind.

How?

It is that little voice in your head…and mine that chatters constantly nonstop.

What stories do you tell yourself?

When I was young, my stories were purely imagination. But when I integrated myself at school and saw how different I was from others, my stories changed.

"It's hard! I'm afraid! I can't do it! I'm not good enough!"

These were stories I told myself about myself by observing the world around me. In my home, at school, with relatives and friends.

How these stories are made up depends solely on how you were brought up in your early years.

For me, I was born into a life of fear, always needing to prove my worth. I constantly felt that I wasn't good enough. I witnessed and experienced turbulence and violence in my home. No child should ever be exposed to such situations. Or should they? To learn and grow?

I AM who I AM

My childhood experiences scared me and wrecked my life. To survive and overcome this breakdown, I turned to journaling to quiet my mind and to express my feelings of sadness and grief. To find who I AM.

For many years, I have searched the world around me for answers to my deepest darkest questions. And often, I let my ego take over to control the stories I told myself, ignoring how I felt within me.

My journey to healing was a long hard road travelled; however, journaling showed me a pattern in my behavior, through my words and actions. It gave me a place to start searching for answers and connecting to each piece of the puzzle in my life until I envisioned the full picture. To look within.

What I discovered was an abundance of pure magical energy, my innate gift and talents; everything I ever needed to live a fulfilled life was within me. It was through my experiences in life and taking time to journal that brought me on a path of self-discovery. Wow!

I was in my teens when I first started journaling and didn't know what to write because my mind was too busy. So I wrote my thoughts. I rekindled all my actions and experiences into words and the imprints of my handwriting showed me a pattern in my life, what I had missed out during all the chaos. What I learned is when I reacted to experiences in my external environment, it really was a trigger from something I had experienced in my past that impacted my memories.

I found this pattern from going back to my journals and reading them. It helped me change my thoughts and my life.

There are days when I just got stuck, fear paralyzed me. And I could not write anything. There is nothing wrong with that. If you ever feel that way, simply take a deep breath and go with the flow. Don't push too hard till you break. Surrender...and do whatever it takes to move on.

My journal gave evidence of what I needed to heal in my life from my traumatic childhood. And I learned to align my thoughts to listen to my deepest desires and to go through my emotions, to process without judgement, to quiet my mind, the inner critic, and to connect to my true feelings.

When I focused and reflected on my actions and behavior, I realized no one had control over them but me. So I chose to take action in my life to make things right.

I moved from always pleasing others to finding the truth of my identity. Who I AM.

You are worthy of a life full of hope and dreams with opportunities to experience the fullness of life and how it feels to be alive.

Journaling allowed me to pay attention to my deepest desires to heal my past. Through writing and releasing the energy of my past, I awakened my spirit of adventure.

My whole life changed as I wrote down my intentions to live the life I wanted to experience.

I looked into my future, created the life I wanted to live.

You have the ability to change your story anytime. Don't live your life by default and accept what you get given. For you are the explorer on a journey to discover the person you were born to be.

Know this: you have everything you need to sustain life within you.

The world is a beautiful place and when you truly accept who you are, you see it reflected back into your life.

* * *

Alison Laverty is a multimedia expert and author of her memoir, **Meant to Be**. *Raised amid family violence, as a teenager, Alison contemplated suicide. Homeless and shunned by society at age seventeen, Alison and her mother struggled to survive. Chronic illness and a near-death experience led to her journey of self-discovery. Guided by her mother's gentle whispers, Alison followed her dreams. Accepting her weaknesses and fears as hidden strengths, Alison believes that forgiveness begins with self. Alison lives with her Aussie bloke and their two mischievous possums in Brisbane, in the Sunshine State of Queensland, Australia. You can learn about Alison at www.alisonlaverty.com.*

Get Into Your Storytelling Routine

Developing a storytelling journal style is a lot of fun, and it can change your life. You can start slowly and gradually develop a practice that is authentically YOU. Here is a snapshot of how you can develop your journaling storytelling routine.

Start by making it easy. Journal for between five and 15 minutes. More is fine, but don't put pressure on yourself to go beyond what feels comfortable.

You can work your way into it by first writing about things you want to do during the day, or things you want to have happen during the day. This can be a nice relaxing part of your morning routine.

In the evening, you may want to grab your pen and pad for a few minutes and write about what happened during the day for which you're grateful. During this time you may also want to look back on good things that have happened throughout your life and add them to the gratitude portion of your journal.

You may also want to write about bad things that have happened to you that led to positive life lessons and give thanks for these moments as well.

Again, start slow and don't expect too much from yourself. Go easy and just celebrate the fact that you've started this new routine in your life. Do this, and you'll begin to feel positive, vibrant energy flowing through your soul.

As this journaling practice grows and becomes part of your regular routine, begin to write with clarity and detail about the things you WANT to manifest in your life. Give thanks and gratitude for them, even before they show up in your life.

Why did I capitalize the word *WANT*? Because a lot of people struggle with this word. They struggle with the feeling that to manifest something they have to *deserve* it or *be worthy* of it. Guess what—you don't have to go through this mental anguish and beat up on yourself.

It's OK to simply want something.

Wanting something doesn't make you selfish or self-centered. It just means you're clear on what you desire.

Now, don't eliminate the feeling that you have to deserve something or be worthy of it, and then simply replace this with a belief that says you have to *work hard and EARN it*. There's no need to mess with your head this way.

One more time—it's OK to simply WANT something.

Alison Laverty tells me the main thing she now writes about in her journal is what she'd like to manifest in her life and what she is grateful for. She also maintains a section in her journal where she records what she did that day or the night before.

If you choose to journal to create better stories in your life, organizing your journal in a similar manner may work for you. But feel free to use this structure as a guideline and shape your journaling practice in a way that is authentically YOU.

I have spoken with many people who have followed this journaling path, and many report that when they write about what they WANT in a calm, relaxed state, what they want often manifests itself within a few days.

Others report that when they write about what they WANT in a state of anxiousness or impatience, what they desire seems to elude them continually.

My firm belief is that when you write about that which you want to manifest, you create much less resistance when you are in a calm, cool state. The way to create this relaxed state is to focus on *what* you want and *why* you want it. Let the Universe handle the *how* and the *when*, and you'll find it's much easier to stay cool and calm.

Do this, and you'll be amazed at how what you desire comes to you in ways you would have never imagined.

Don't Put a Timeline on Things

This point ties into what I stated in the few previous paragraphs, but it's worth reiterating. Don't put a timeline on manifesting what you want. This creates pressure, and pressure creates energetic resistance.

Instead, journal about what you desire as if you already have it. Don't drive yourself nuts by being in a big rush. Once again, focus on the *what* and the *why*, and let the Universe manage the *how* and the *when*.

Alison Laverty believes that at the end of the day, it's all about surrender and being detached from the outcome. I agree with her completely.

When you surrender, what you desire and focus on will happen to you in the most unbelievable ways. And it may be even bigger and better than you ever would have expected!

And as you begin to manifest what you desire, you'll feel a tremendous sense of certainty that YOU made it all happen!

Now, I'm very aware that remaining in a cool, calm state of relaxed anticipation can be difficult when you want to manifest something wonderful. So let me ask you a question.

Have you ever grown and nurtured a vegetable garden?

If you have, you know the process. If you haven't, you're probably familiar with the process. In a nutshell, you plant seeds and over time those seeds sprout. Nurture your garden with water and sunshine, and next thing you know, you're growing vegetables.

You don't get uptight or anxious with this process because you TRUST IT!

When you plant seeds, you don't run out to your garden three days later and start yelling at the ground because your vegetables haven't grown yet. You don't lie awake at night staring at the ceiling feeling stressed that you weren't able to serve fresh tomatoes from your brand-new garden that night.

You don't do this for two reasons: 1) you're not insane, and 2) you trust the evolving nature of the garden-growing process.

When it comes to manifesting want you WANT, treat your life as you would your vegetable garden and things will work out just fine.

There Are No Limits!

Journaling to tell a better story about your life comes with one massive benefit: there are no limits! The potential is huge, and you can create anything and everything in your life as long as you let go of your past.

You can literally create a new life out of nothing.

Journal about button-size intentions, and you can create a button-size life. Journal about castle-size dreams, and you can manifest a castle-size life. One isn't any better than the other. It's up to YOU.

You can create a new life free from being trapped. Do this by putting your focus on where you are now at this moment and pour it out into your journal. From this flow you can shift gears and simply write, "My life is this way now, but I intend to make it *this* way."

With this thought, you can begin to detail your vision and intentions. Remember, where attention goes, the energy flows. Or, as Tony Robbins always says, "What you focus on expands in your life." Write about your intentions, vision, and new life story in sharp, crystal-clear detail. Live it, feel, breathe it, smell it.

Even before you manifest this vision, writing about it with such certainty will make you feel amazing!

You can close out the past and write and create anything you want. Again, the only limits are the ones you impose on yourself. So just say, "There are no limits!"

At a minimum, when you are journaling your better life story, simply using your imagination will make you feel fantastic because you're focusing on what's new and good in your life—instead of what's old and bad.

So journal the story you want your life to be. And remember, there are NO limits!

The Lesson in All This

When I asked Alison Laverty the lesson she's learned through journaling to create a new life story, she said, "The lesson I learned is that even though I make mistakes, they make me stronger. And now when I move forward from a mistake, I know exactly what to do."

Another valuable lesson you'll learn through this form of journaling is finding out who you are at your core. You'll discover that you are special in your own unique way, and that the way you assemble your words and thoughts may be different from that of other people you know, but that they are original to you. And they are perfectly YOU!

This self-acceptance will help you beat down your inner critic. You'll be empowered to peel away the layers that have been placed on you by the world. As you peel and shed these layers, you'll discover the essence of who YOU are.

The biggest lesson you'll learn is there's a real treasure in the midst of all your journaling. And the treasure is that you get to know the true YOU, and who YOU are. As a result, you'll become much more comfortable with YOU, and so much more grateful for YOU.

As Alison Laverty pointed out to me, you'll get to know what your hopes, your desires, and your dreams are. This will put you in a wonderful place where you can plan your life anew through journaling.

In a sense, your writing will enable you to wipe your slate clean. Then you will have the freedom to fill it with EVERYTHING you want.

It's like a blank canvas upon which you can paint your new life picture!

Your Journaling Prompt

Creating a new life story for yourself through journaling is a magical adventure. To get started, simply grab your pad and pen and write this down: "My name is _____, and I want to create something different in my life."

Every journey begins with your first step, and this simple step can be the first you take in using journaling to create a new life for yourself. From here, take this next step and keep going!

Express how you feel about your current life and why you want to change it. Go into great detail about behaviors, beliefs, and patterns you'd like to remove from your life.

Don't hold anything back!

Relax and breathe as you go through this process. Take your time. There's no rush. Enjoy it. Breathe and be free. Whatever your feelings may be, allow them to flow forth from you in great detail. It's just you and your pad and pen, so you have nothing to hide.

It's time to set yourself FREE!

Give yourself several days, weeks, or months to do this. Be thorough and let it all out. All of it! Don't hold anything back. If you stick with it and let your honest feelings come forth, you'll slowly begin to remove negative experiences, patterns, habits, and beliefs from your life. You'll know you've released them when you find you no longer focus on them.

With this negativity out of the way, there will be an abundance of room for new energy to flow into your life, which is essential to creating your new life story.

Attitude of Gratitude

A great way to get this new energy flowing into your life is to take another step in your journey and begin a gratitude journal. Write about things for which you are grateful each and every day. As you do, you'll find it feels natural and energizing to begin giving thanks for things you want as if you already have them!

As you build *gratitude journaling momentum*, it won't feel like a stretch to show gratitude for things, people, and opportunities you wish to manifest.

Starting your gratitude journal is easy. It can be as simple as writing, "I am grateful I have this notepad and pen. And I am grateful I am journaling." Keep it simple. Give thanks for your meals, or your health, or the clothes on your back.

Start simple and get in a groove. Don't put too much pressure on yourself.

By doing this, you'll slowly begin to accept yourself and love yourself more. You will build up energy and unstoppable momentum.

However, if you try to bite off too much too fast, you'll procrastinate.

So keep it simple and slowly build up your gratitude muscle! You can do this! And when you do, you'll be amazed at how things for which you're giving gratitude begin to show up in your life in ways you could never have imagined.

Next thing you know, you're creating a new life story for yourself!

> *"Samuel Johnson said, 'Adversity introduces a man to himself.' I think journaling introduces a man or woman to themselves. And sometimes we can have a strong or complicated reaction to this person we're being introduced to."*

> **—Dennis Palumbo, M.A., MFT**, Author and Psychotherapist

Chapter 8

Design Your Future

One of my tribe members is award-winning copywriter and consultant Casey Demchak. Casey has written marketing copy for dozens of books that have become Amazon bestsellers.

He's been writing since he was a kid, and he spent his 20s pursuing a screenwriting career in Hollywood. Along the way he also worked for a while as a story analyst for Ron Howard and Anson Williams, who of course played Richie and Potsie on the classic '70s TV show *Happy Days*.

In addition to his passion for writing, Casey Demchak grew up playing baseball in California. He loved it. As a kid, he played every day he could, and he was a good hitter!

He also was a very good catcher, made the all-star team every year, and collected a bunch of trophies. But early on, Casey says he had one thing working against him in the eyes of his coaches: he was too easygoing.

However, one day when he was 11 years old, he drove a ball up the right-centerfield alley and slid into second with a double that drove in two runs. He pumped his fist, pounded his chest, and got really enthusiastic.

His coach was a wonderful man named Gene Baxter. Mr. Baxter took notice of Casey's excitement, and after the game he pulled Casey aside and said, "I saw how you got really excited after you hit that double." Casey quickly replied, "Heck yeah, I drove in two runs. It felt great."

Coach Baxter then said something that changed Casey's life:

> *"When you get into the batter's box,*
> *act as if you've already hit a double.*
> *If you do, you'll hit a lot more doubles."*

This was great advice. Casey tells me he went on to hit a lot of doubles over the years, and it was because he conditioned himself to feel the excitement of hitting a double every time he stepped into the batter's box. The key phrase here is: "act as if." If you listen to Tony Robbins and other self-development leaders, you will hear this phrase a lot.

"Journal As If" You Already Have It

When Casey began his journaling practice, he didn't forget the great advice he got years earlier from his Little League coach. He is also a big Tony Robbins fan, so the phrase "act as if" remained close to Casey's heart.

The basic principle being that you shouldn't wait until you've made money to walk, talk, and act like you have financial abundance. Instead, walk, talk, and act "as if" you already have financial abundance...and then it will flow to you.

Of course, this simple principle can be applied to every aspect of your life, not just finances. Being a writer, Casey took it a little further and believed that his life would become the story he told about himself.

This concept became the theme of Casey's daily journaling practice. Before "acting as if" he already had what he desired, Casey decided to "journal as if" he already had what he desired.

He calls this practice *affirmative journaling*.

Casey is an active member of my CreateWriteNow.com tribe. As a contributor to my blog, he wrote a guest post titled *The Power of Affirmative Journaling*, in which he details this daily expressive writing practice. Here is his post:

The Power of Affirmative Journaling

By Casey Demchak—Copywriter & Consultant

The first 100-story building was not designed and built by someone with a 50-story imagination. Now, I don't know who this person was, but I'm certain before this building existed, the designer focused a lot of thought on it, and wrote about it by putting pen to paper (*no personal computers back then*).

By 1) focusing his or her thoughts on this 100-story building, and by 2) writing about it, the building's designer hardwired the feeling of creating the building into his or her mind before it existed in physical form.

These two steps were essential to taking the vision of a 100-story building and turning it into a living reality.

So why not think equally big and apply this simple two-step process to your life? I do! I call it *affirmative journaling*…and it's a huge part of my morning routine.

It works like this: Instead of writing about what has happened in my life, I journal the story of what I want my life to become. In rich detail, I describe what I want to manifest in my life—but I write about it as if I already have it.

For example, I never write, "*I want…*" Instead, I always write, "*I have…*" I do this because when you write, feel, and act as if all you desire is already yours…it comes to you much more quickly.

Here is my easy-to-follow process.

Think Big and Be Affirmative

If you think about it, it takes no more energy to envision a button than it does a castle. In other words, thinking big requires no more energy than thinking small. So I choose to think big!

When I was an 11-year-old baseball player, I had a coach tell me that if

I stepped into the batter's box feeling like I've already hit a double—I'd hit more doubles. Sage advice to receive at such a young age…and my coach was right.

After getting this great advice, I never waited to hit a double to feel great about myself. Instead, I trained myself to feel as if I had already smashed the ball up the right-center field alley as I stepped up to home plate. This made me incredibly energized and confident. As you might expect…I hit more doubles.

This is the frame of mind I settle into each morning as I do my affirmative journaling. I envision everything I want in my life and allow myself to feel as if I've already attained it. Then I start writing!

Pen to Paper is the Key

When I was in college I had a geography teacher who allowed us to bring in one 4x6" note card loaded with "cheat" notes into class for each test. Naturally, I hand wrote as many notes as I could—as small as I could—on my 4" x 6" cheat sheet.

As I wrote my notes, I focused and concentrated and made the most of every available speck of space on my trusty cheat sheet.

But then a funny thing happened. By concentrating so hard when I hand wrote my microscopic cheat notes…I didn't need to look at them when I took the test!

By focusing so intensely as I hand wrote my notes, they became hard-wired in my brain. This illustrates the power of pen-to-paper writing! This is why I handwrite my affirmative journal.

Writing by hand forces you to focus on each letter of every word, and every word of every sentence. This drives your thoughts, feelings, and desires into your mind. Your mind will then pepper your intuition with actions you MUST take to make your thoughts your reality.

Pen-to-paper writing forces you to focus much more than tapping your fingers on a keyboard. And when your mind is more focused, it will fuel you with thoughts and actions you can take to manifest your desires.

This is why even though I own two computers, I do all my affirmative journaling with my favorite pen on yellow legal pads…and I always will.

Focus Your Thoughts

Motivation and behavior expert Tony Robbins often says, "What you focus on expands in your life." When I take an honest look at *my* life, I can say with certainty that this has been true (for better and for worse).

For this reason, the next step in my affirmative journaling process is to focus throughout the day on what I've written in the morning. I do this because I'm certain my life will become the story I tell about myself.

And again, I always tell my story in the affirmative, *as if* it's already happened.

For example, I never write or think about how I'd like great new clients to come into my business. Instead, I give thanks and gratitude for the great clients that have turned to me for my help…and then they appear. It never fails.

This is how I've thrived in my copywriting business for 17 years…and this is how I met Mari L. McCarthy!

Forget About Good Grammar and All That!

Lastly, no one is going to read your journal except you. So don't worry about good grammar or spelling mistakes. Just write in a conversational tone that is authentically you. Relax and be yourself!

You can do this!

In fact, if you can handwrite a shopping list, you have all the skills you need to master affirmative journaling! So why not get started today!

* * *

Casey Demchak is an author, speaker, and recognized expert at writing highly effective sales copy for coaches, authors, and B2B corporate clients. He has written sales and marketing copy for dozens of authors/coaches who have achieved bestseller and international bestseller status with Amazon.com. You can learn more about him at www.CaseyDemchak.com.

Where Your Attention Goes—the Energy Flows

When I first read Casey's blog post I was very intrigued for a couple reasons. First, it speaks to the power of focus. I am a big believer that where your attention goes, the energy flows. And when your energy gets flowing in a certain direction, you tend to build momentum in that direction.

Think about it: people who expend a lot of energy talking about their relationship problems tend to have more relationship problems.

Did you ever have a relative or friend who always complained about household appliances and things breaking down in their home right when they were about to start getting ahead financially? "Something is always breaking. If it's not one thing, it's another."

If you knew someone like this, you probably also noticed they seemed to stay stuck in this loop. It comes back to focus. As I've said, what you focus on expands in your life. So be very thoughtful about what you focus on in your life.

As Casey Demchak demonstrates with the affirmative-journaling practice he outlined, daily expressive writing is a fantastic way to focus on what you want your life to be. It's a great way to use your writing to "act as if."

Nothing significant happens in your life without you first imagining it. Before you get the better job, you first imagine having a better job. Before you get new wooden floors and granite countertops, you first imagine having them. Before you meet your soulmate, you imagine being with him or her first.

However, sometimes we make the mistake of always seeing these things as "someday" items. As a result, they can seem elusive, because we always think about them as being events off in the distance that will happen "someday."

Well, there really is no such thing as yesterday or tomorrow. There's only today! All we've got is RIGHT NOW! Every moment we live in our lives is RIGHT NOW.

So why wait until you get the better job, or the wooden floors and the granite countertops, or the soulmate, to start feeling fantastic. Journal about having these things in your life, and you'll feel better RIGHT NOW.

When you practice affirmative journaling, you're not writing about the past or the future. You're taking things from the future and pulling them into your life today! Along with this comes the feeling of already having them, and this makes you feel fantastic.

Remember, when you focus on what you don't have, you energetically create resistance to getting what you want.

However, when you feel and "act as if" you already have what you desire, you eliminate resistance, and things flow your way much easier.

Every wonder why people with money tend to have an easier time making even more money than people who are poor? It's because people with money always feel "as if" they *have* money so energetically, it's much easier for even more financial abundance to flow to them.

You can say the same thing about career success, health, and romance. When you feel as though you have what you desire, it's easier for more of it to come your way.

This is the magic of affirmative journaling.

Use Your Journal to Tell a Better Life Story

The second thing that excites me about Casey Demchak's affirmative journaling practice is how simple it can be. When you break it down, all Casey is doing each day is writing a better-feeling story about his life.

You can do the same thing.

If "acting as if" or believing "where your attention goes the energy flows" feels a little tricky or awkward to you, take an even more simplified approach to affirmative journaling.

Use your journal to tell a very compelling story about your life. We all love stories. Think about the people you find to be among your favorite to be around at social events or family gatherings. Chances are, they tell good stories.

We all tell stories about our past. We can all spin a yarn about something funny that happened in high school, or how nervous we were on the first day of our first big job after college.

They may not be novels or professionally crafted screenplays, but we all tell stories. This is how easy affirmative journaling can be.

Just think about how you want your life to be and write the story of your life each day "as if" your life is already that way.

Don't write the story of how you hope to go on a beach vacation to Santa Barbara, California, next summer. Write a journal entry about how it feels to be on the beach in Santa Barbara. Feel it, breathe it, and write about it as if it's happening right now.

Don't write the story of how tough it is to pay your bills, and that you will feel better down the road when you make more money.

Instead, write in the affirmative. Write about how you feel knowing that financial freedom is your birthright. Write about the satisfaction you feel knowing you're secure because money flows to you in abundance.

Write that story for yourself.

Don't write the story of how you never seem to meet a soulmate with whom you can have a loving relationship. Instead, write about how wonderful it feels to be spending each day with the person of your dreams. Write about how joyous it feels to have them beside you in everything you do.

Don't write about how you can't seem to lose those 10 pounds you gained over the holidays. Tell a different story. Write about how vibrant you feel because you're following eating and exercise habits that have you feeling better than ever before.

The Lesson in All This

If you put out a lot of energy that says, "I have more money," guess what you are going to attract? More money.

If you put out a lot of energy that says, "I am with my soulmate," guess what you are going to attract? Your soulmate.

If you put out a lot of energy that says, "I have better health," guess what you are going to attract? Better health.

Your life becomes the story you tell about yourself. So use your journaling to tell a great one. Be affirmative. Be positive, be BOLD, and dream BIG. As Casey Demchak says in his post, the first 100-story building wasn't built by someone with a 50-story imagination.

It's absolutely great to ask for things and truly believe they will come to you. In fact, doing so is essential. But take it one step further and journal as if you already have them.

Make things immediate. Be affirmative. Don't just talk about what you want to have. Give gratitude and thanks that they are already here. Journal about them as if they have arrived and let yourself feel the joy of having them. This what people mean when they say:

"Enjoy the journey, not just the destination."

When you **"act as if," "think as if," speak as if," and JOURNAL as if**, you will be able to manifest what you desire more rapidly.

This doesn't mean it's going to happen overnight, and it doesn't mean you're not going to feel frustration. But it does mean you are putting yourself on a course that can lead you to that which you want most in your life.

Your Journaling Prompt

Your prompt for this chapter is to start an affirmative-journaling practice! There are several ways to get going. Feel free to choose one that is comfortable for you.

The most obvious way is to follow the outline provided by Casey Demchak. Just grab a pen and paper and do it!

However, you may be at a point in your life when journaling about your daily activities, thoughts, and emotions is important to you. If this is the case, consider dedicating just a portion of your daily writing-routine time to affirmative journaling.

For example, you can conclude each writing session by crafting a paragraph or two about your new life story. Or you could dedicate a third or a half of your writing time to affirmative journaling.

It's up to you. Some writers even choose to dedicate one or two days a week to affirmative journaling, while recording their daily thoughts and emotions the remaining days of the week.

Create an affirmative-journaling routine that feels right to you. However, I highly recommend you incorporate this practice into your writing routine.

When you write the life story you want to live as if you are already living it, you will be amazed at how energized and joyous you feel.

Your mind and soul will be fueled with ideas you can implement and actions you can take to make the vision you have for your life your new everyday reality.

As you live, breathe, walk, talk, and journal "as if" all you desire is already in your life, resistance and doubt will leave your being, a new YOU will emerge, and positive energy will flow through every cell in your body. This is when magic happens! So grab your pen and paper and go for it!

> *"Journaling can play a huge role in manifesting the life you want. If you want to manifest a partner, write about that partner every day as if they're already in your life. Or write to them as if you're writing a letter to them."*

> —**Jenetta Haim**, Founder of Stressfree Management®;
> Lifestyle and Health Management Expert

Chapter 9

Manifest a Life You Love

Cheryl Sutherland has amazing energy and is a most appreciated member of the Create Write Now tribe. Spend a few moments speaking with Cheryl, and you will immediately feel inspired and energized.

In the previous two chapters, I wrote about how Alison Laverty and Casey Demchak use journaling to move from where they are to where they want to be. As you know by now, journaling is an amazing tool for telling and creating a new life story for yourself.

Cheryl Sutherland is another example of a vibrant, gifted person who believes you can manifest a life you love by using your natural power to create. A power many people are not aware they have. For Cheryl, harnessing this power includes staying committed to a journaling practice that has moved mountains in her life.

On one hand, Cheryl's mission of creating a life she loves through journaling is similar to the techniques used by Alison and Casey. But on the other hand, Cheryl's story and approach to journaling is uniquely her own and believe me when I tell you...it is very POWERFUL!

Cheryl is also an example of someone who didn't automatically take to journaling. She resisted it for a period of time, and her journaling practice took a while to evolve. But once she found her groove, the floodgates completely opened up for her.

Cheryl is a wonderful example of someone who gave herself permission to allow her journaling practice to take shape over time. She set HER own pace and created HER own unique rituals and routines.

The journey Cheryl took to develop and refine her journaling routine is best described in a blog post she wrote for CreateWriteNow.com. I am pleased to share it with you here.

How Journaling Helped Me Manifest a Life I Love

By Cheryl Sutherland—Founder, PleaseNotes.com

I first got asked to start journaling at different personal-growth seminars I went to. Facing my fears, crying over past trauma, pushing through fears… easy…journaling was the WORST THING EVER. It was a supreme level of vulnerability that I didn't let myself go to until I decided to change my life.

It took me a very long time to get into journaling. I inherently had so much resistance to it for all the reasons journaling is so good for you.

1. Everything you write is real.
2. You have to be honest with yourself, and you know if you're not.

When you have thoughts, ideas, emotions and judgments, they can change, shift, be forgotten or rewritten. You can justify bad behavior from yourself and others, or even lose a memory entirely. When you write it on the page, it gives it life and makes it 100% real.

There's a quote by Marianne Williamson often attributed to Nelson Mandela that states, "Our deepest fear is not that we are inadequate. Our deepest fear is that we are powerful beyond measure. It is our Light, not our Darkness, that most frightens us."

At the time, my deepest fear was to step out of the shadows, to create something that I would attribute to myself, something that has been waiting for me to say yes to. I just needed to be brave enough to shine a light internally and when I found what I had been searching for, not turn my back.

I got into journaling when I was at a crossroads in my life. Like a lot of people, I was working somewhere I didn't feel valued or valuable and didn't know what to do. I took a leap and quit that job, so I could work on myself. I started reading a ton, decided who I really was by creating and practicing affirmations and then picked up the pen and got to journaling.

Through journaling, I was able to understand my feelings, my inherent value, and myself. I was able to see the chinks in my armor where I had chosen not to look. I was able to work out feelings and have real conversations with only the judgment or opinions would come from myself. I was able to see why I had been blocking myself for so long and decided that I was worthy; I had value and gifts to share.

One thing I always look back on is my ideal scene for a business. I didn't know what it was; however, I wrote out attributes of it. That I wanted to be able to work from anywhere from my laptop, that it was a product, that it helped people, that it was accessible to anyone, that I felt amazing and expansive doing the business, and that it made a difference in people's lives. When I got the idea for sticky notes with a different affirmation on each page, I was able to go over that checklist in my head, so quickly I knew that this was exactly what I was looking for, and I didn't let it go.

I've used this ideal scene technique to attract living situations, friends, and business partners. I feel like journaling is the equivalent to a signal box booster to the Universe, and if used with love, joy, and heart, you can always manifest the highest and best.

* * *

Cheryl Sutherland is an entrepreneur, speaker, optimism coach, and lover of cupcakes. She founded PleaseNotes.com to give people tools to transform their lives, and the exercises in her guided journal allow people to get connected with themselves so they can make tangible shifts in their lives. Please visit www.PleaseNotes.com to learn more about her.

Set Your Pace. Go with Your Flow!

What I really admire about Cheryl's approach to journaling is that she doesn't trap herself into a strict routine, and she gives herself the freedom to ride with the tide and go with the flow. If this approach sounds appealing to you, you may want to consider a journaling practice that resembles Cheryl's.

In the morning you may write about what you want to take on that day, and you may provide detail about what you want to have happen. Have fun with this! Be vivid and vibrant as you use your imagination to paint a picture of how you want your day to go.

Don't hold anything back. Remember, your imagination is your primary manifestation tool, so let it rip!

Think back to when you were a child and how you used your imagination with reckless abandon. You placed no limits on yourself and you just went wild with it. Well, who says you can't do that now!

Have fun and go for it! Write in rich detail about all the wonderful things you want to have happen during your day.

Ask Questions. Get Answers.

Later in the day or at night you may want to swing back to your journal if something comes up during your day that you need to figure out. When this happens, it's always a strong idea to confront your issue by premising it with a question.

You can simply ask why your particular issue is an issue at all. Questions are powerful. When you frame your personal issues in the form of questions, and write them down, pen to paper, you'll be astonished at how fast answers come zipping back to you through your intuition.

The key is to listen to your inner voice when it shouts back you. After all, that voice is there for a reason.

For example, if you feel your life is overly cluttered and rushed, you can take out your pad and pen and write down a question such as, "Why has my life become so hectic and rushed?" What can come back to you through your intuition may be something like, "Because you allow other people to make your life that way."

This may prompt you to then write down this question: "What's a simple step I can take that will allow me to take command of the pace at which I live my life?"

Write down this question, and your intuition may scream back at you, "The first step you can take is to check your email three times a day, instead of 33 times a day!"

Writing down questions that revolve around the issues in your tissues can be incredibly powerful if you're open to getting brutally honest answers back through your intuition.

If you haven't tried this, go for it!

Script Your Life

Cheryl Sutherland reports that her journaling practice includes a lot of exercises. One that really fascinates me is called *scripting*.

Scripting is when you write out exactly what you want moments in your life to be like. The idea is simple. Take pen to paper and script life moments in rich detail. Then take several moments to immerse yourself in what you have written.

Don't be shy or feel funny about this part. Get into it! Live the moment you've scripted. Breathe it, visualize it, feel it in your soul, smell it, appreciate it, and make it REAL.

If you're going create your new life story, don't hold anything back. Script it and experience it in your mind and magic will happen.

Think of this exercise as creating your own virtual reality—without having to wear those silly-looking goggles.

Cheryl Sutherland has other innovative journaling exercises I think you'd enjoy. Most of them are in her guided affirmation journal, which you can learn more about here: https://pleasenotes.com/collections/the-guided-affirmation-journal-new.

Allow Yourself to Be Inspired

As I've said, Cheryl Sutherland journals to manifest the life she loves. One thing I admire about Cheryl is she gives herself the freedom to achieve this by journaling in a way that feels right at that moment. In other words, she allows herself to be inspired.

You can do the same!

For example, you may decide to do gratitude journaling on a particular day and really step into it. You may not want to record what you did the day before. Instead, you may go through a period where you want to write in rich detail about that for which you are grateful.

If that's the way the Universal winds are pushing you, go with it!

Cheryl tells me that on a particular day she may feel called upon to write her appreciation for what her business has become, and the type of person *she's* become as a result of it. I love this because she is allowing her inspiration to guide her to whatever cavern she is being called toward.

The lesson here is that you don't always have to set a hardened direction for your journaling practice. Instead, allow yourself to be guided and soak up the joy of how invigorating this can be. When you grab your pen and pad, be open to having your inner voice tap you on the shoulder and say, "This is where we're going today."

Leverage the Power of Focus

A tremendous benefit that stems from this form of journaling is that it gives you the ability to leverage the power of focus. Once again, as Tony Robbins says, "What you focus on expands in your life."

It's great to think about your issues. Thoughts are things and your thoughts are powerful. But when you sit down and write pen-to-paper about an issue, your brain will become very focused on the intricate details of whatever is on your mind.

Thinking and writing requires more focus than thinking alone. So journaling about the issues in your tissues really helps you bring more of what you WANT into your life. The reason this happens is because when you write in detail you gain tremendous clarity about what you want, and this clarity becomes hardwired in your brain.

For example, if you want a new mate, write about who this person is and what this relationship looks like, feels like, smells like, and tastes like. Embrace the experience with all your senses as if it's already in your life. Become very clear with your vision and write about it in vivid detail.

When you are very focused through your writing on what you want and it manifests in your life, you will already be familiar with it. It will be easy to recognize, you'll know what to do with it, and it will feel very satisfying.

Again, the keyword here is *focus*. Remember, your thoughts become things. So focus and write about things that really appeal to YOU.

Need a little help with this? Use the same approach you take when you go to an all-you-can-eat buffet. As you stand before a buffet knowing you can have anything you want, your eyes and thoughts immediately focus on the food items that appeal to you.

However, you don't get annoyed because there are food choices in the buffet you don't want to eat. Instead, you just ignore them.

Take this same approach with your journaling. Put your attention on what appeals to you and the power of focus will make magic happen in your life.

No Judgment. Be Good to Yourself.

The benefits of journaling to manifest the life you want really flow your way when you don't connect any judgment to what you're writing or how long you're writing. In other words, relax and go easy on yourself.

Don't freak out if you don't write at the same time every day for a set period of time. Don't beat up on yourself if you miss a day or spend less time journaling on a particular morning. This makes you uptight and being uptight creates resistance.

Instead, just be thankful and proud you're participating in your journaling process.

In addition, there's a measure of catharsis in writing. These days, we have so much running through our minds, which leads to a mental-energy drain and physical exhaustion that comes with checking your email too often, watching the news too much, or fussing over social media for hours at a time.

In today's constantly connected Wi-Fi-everywhere-you-go society, we tend to have a snowstorm of thoughts zipping around our brains constantly—and this isn't necessarily good for us.

Journaling allows you to break from this grind and create a sense of calm, so you can get clear on what you want. Even when you write about something bad that happened during your day, journaling empowers you to release it from your system, so you can focus more energy on good stuff to come!

The Lesson in All This

The lesson here is simple. You can have everything that you want, as long as you decide you are worthy of it. And as I've said, the easy way around the "am I worthy?" issue is to just decide you WANT something.

I'll say it again: it's perfectly fine to just WANT something.

If you give yourself permission to just want something, it makes it much easier to feel as if you already have it. If you still feel a little guilty about the "want" issue, keep this in mind: the more you have, the more you can give.

Bottom line: you can use journaling to help manifest anything you want. Putting pen to paper gives you the power to paint the picture of what you want your life to become. This picture can be as rich in detail as you want it to be.

Most important, you can do this from a place of ease. Creating the life you want doesn't have to be about strife, struggle, or "earning" it. It can simply be about using your focus and your imagination to create it.

The best part is, YOU get to define YOUR version of success, fun, and happiness.

Your Journaling Prompt

Some of the writing prompts in this book are a little more involved, and some are simple and to the point. This one is simple and to the point! An easy process you can follow to manifest a life you love through journaling is this: start by journaling your answer to the question "What do I appreciate?"

Set a timer and allow yourself to write freely for five or 10 minutes...or even two minutes...and just let your appreciation flow. The key is to focus your full attention on what you're feeling, with little attention paid to the mechanics of how you're writing.

Remember, this is your journal. Nobody is going to edit or grade it. So don't worry about how organized your writing is or whether you're repeating the same descriptive words. Just let your thoughts flow naturally and go with it.

As you journal about things for which you feel appreciation, a funny thing will happen. You'll begin to feel fantastic! You'll feel freer, more positive, more energetic, and unstoppable.

Let this feeling build and swell within you.

Then, begin to do the same free-flowing journaling about things you want to manifest in your life. Describe them in detail. Be specific about why you want them, and why you already appreciate them.

Have fun with this! Let your thoughts go wild. Be free. Use your imagination and don't set any boundaries. Over time you'll feel unstoppable. And when you reach the point of feeling unstoppable, enjoy it and take it very seriously. *Because you are unstoppable!*

> *"When you journal, especially when you ask questions, answers seem to come flying at you through your intuition. Journaling helps you realize you have more answers within you than you are aware of. And sometimes the answers you receive through journaling are a wonderful surprise."*

—Dennis Palumbo, M.A., MFT, Author and Psychotherapist

Chapter 10

Manage Your Mind

Has the Information Age overwhelmed your nervous system? Do you often feel that information is coming at you so fast from so many directions that you can never feel fully calm and relaxed?

If you're like nearly every single person I talk to, the answer to these two questions is probably "Yes." If my assumption is correct, take comfort in the fact that you're not alone. As you'll discover in this chapter, journaling is a tremendous tool for protecting yourself from information overload, and I am going to show you how to wield this tool with a lot of power!

But first, take a deep breath and allow yourself to acknowledge that information overload is indeed real, and that at times it adds a lot of undue stress and strain to your life.

The root cause of information overload can be neatly summed up in one simple word: *smartphone.*

It's not a stretch to say that the smartphone has radically turned our civilization on its head. Because of smartphones, life seems to be accelerating at a faster and faster pace that is nearly impossible to keep up with.

At our fingertips we now have the amazing ability to access and communicate information to thousands of people at once. However, at the same time, thousands of people have the ability to zip, zap, email, and tweet information at us constantly.

You live with this 24/7, and this never-ending stream of information can completely boggle your mind. On one hand you complain about it, but on the other hand you must admit that you may have allowed yourself to become addicted to it.

However, if you've reached the point where you'd like it to all slow down and become more manageable for your mind, body, and soul...keep reading. Because I am going to show you how to use journaling to make the world move at whatever speed YOU choose.

The first thing you can do is articulate your boundaries. You actually do have a choice when it comes to how much information you're going to allow to come flying at you through your smartphone, laptop, tablet, or desktop.

You also get to choose how often you're going to check your email. Remember, you may be checking it five or 10 times an hour right now (or more), but it's not because somebody else is making you do it. It's because YOU choose to.

A powerful way to set your e-boundaries is to clearly articulate them in your journal. Be open and honest with yourself when you do this.

You can start by writing honest answers to questions you must confront if you're serious about managing information overload. Some of these questions could include:

- Am I addicted to email and/or my phone?
- Do I hop on social-media platforms even though I know deep down inside I need a break?
- Does social media drain my mental energy and/or make me mad?
- Does how many Likes my last Facebook post received make or break my day?
- Am I venturing into the "e-world" too often to feed some hidden need for attention or approval?

There's no right or wrong answers to these questions. But it's important that you journal honest answers to them, and any others you can think of. Remember, no one is going to read your journal but you, so be honest and authentic with yourself.

After you have journaled honest answers to your initial list of questions, you can dig a little deeper and answer these three additional questions:

1. What can I do to leverage the flow of information coming at me so it stimulates my energy, instead of draining it?
2. What can I do to control the flow of information coming at me so it doesn't push and pull me around?
3. What can I do to make information flow to me at a rhythm and pace that is comfortable for ME?

Journaling can be the therapist who helps you avoid information overload and information addiction. My good friend and colleague Casey Demchak went through this exercise and he came up with a simple line one morning while he was journaling: "New-school tools, but at an old-school pace."

Writing this simple slogan down in his journal served as his guide for creating information boundaries that work for HIM. For example, Casey tells me this slogan inspired him to check his email just three times a day, instead of 20 times a day. In addition, he now spends 30 minutes a day on social media instead of two or three hours.

After making these changes, Casey reports he hasn't missed out on a thing. His life is still whole and complete, he gets all the information he needs, and he is much calmer and more relaxed.

Journaling about your social media, email, and online habits will help you make healthier choices.

For example, you can grab your journal first thing every morning instead of your phone. This one simple change can empower you to become more connected to a deep inner relationship with yourself, instead of a world you rarely actually come in contact with.

Think about it. How often do the events on your phone or on the news actually impact your life? Yet how much time do you spend thinking about these events? Does doing this increase your energy, or drain it?

Bottom line: "online overwhelm" is real, and I am here to remind you that journaling is a tremendous way to filter out a lot of the crap that is overstimulating your central nervous system.

The Information Age you now live in moves at warp speed, which makes it more important than ever to discover...or rediscover...the relaxed state of mindfulness that journaling brings into your life.

My good friend and Create Write Now tribe member Will Donnelly shared a beautiful blog post with us on this topic that you can find on CreateWriteNow.com. I am also proud to share it with you here.

Information (Age) Overload? Grab a Journal and Write

By Will Donnelly

Most of us are now constantly overrun with information, and our minds are discovering the downside to the "Information Age." It's never been easier to get mentally foggy and enmeshed in our daily obligations and distractions, while slowly letting go of our deepest and most important desires. Too many of our lives, unfortunately, get frittered away by detail, as Thoreau says, and the price for this is great.

The philosopher Plato long ago said "Know thyself," and few paths are as effective as the simple practice of mindfulness. We get hooked on patterns of belief about a particular story we have been telling ourselves, such as "There's never enough money" or "Love is impossible to find," etc., whether or not these stories are actually true. Using mindfulness, we pay attention to who we are at any given moment to look for patterns that are either causing or easing suffering.

Keeping a journal can play a significant role in our self-awareness. Journaling can help us see patterns that may or may not be helpful in our lives and allow us to make changes if we see fit to do so. By journaling, we can grow to trust ourselves, to glean the wisdom from the tingly feeling in our gut, or the heaviness in our hearts.

We journal to gather the courage to move forward in life based on a deeply felt sensation, a more honest guttural feeling of "YES!" We let the colors of our darkness out onto a page, and often find that it's actually not so terrible after all. And when it is terrible, we can face our challenges with clarity and intention.

We journal because it is cathartic. We journal year after year because writing honestly feels raw and truthful, even though not all of it is good. Most of it, the mental chatter of the monkey mind just comes and goes.

Each day's pages are an uncovering, a chipping away at the layers of bull crap that hide the stunning jewel of our hearts. It's heavy under our mental BS. And as the pages and words and tears flow, misunderstandings of ourselves and the world around us get diffused along the way.

So: write. Write every day if you can. Write because words are like a link, a collective arm-hold from across years and cultures. Write because your story needs to be told and understood. Write because bit by bit you can make some sense out of a world that seems to make little or no sense. Write so you can steer your boat, drive in a direction that makes sense to you, ground yourself on solid earth. Write because it just feels so damned good to write, to let the cat out of the bag, to realize there is no bag in the first place. Write to realize all the stories we tell ourselves have consequences, and we can change our stories, and in doing so, heal our lives.

If you are ready to be fully alive, or if you are feeling stuck or over-emotional, or if you need clarity in your life, start journaling. It'll be your BFF, a friend for life. It's actually really easy to begin, and here are three tips to help you engage your self-study practice tomorrow morning:

Grab a journal

Head to your local drug store and find a $4 journal. Get a spiral bound school notebook and a favorite pen, and put them in your nightstand drawer, ready for action. Or get a fancy-boots journal and expensive pen, whatever works for you.

Commit to 10 minutes each morning

To start the process, give yourself five, 10 or 15 minutes each morning. Before you get out of bed to start your day, after you have just awakened, simply grab your journal and write. Commit to a reasonable time that will make sense to your schedule. At the very least, commit to a minimum time of five or 10 minutes. But also be open—if the spirit calls you and your schedule allows, write until you are "done."

Let It flow

Just write in a stream of consciousness. You're not trying to impress anyone, justify your thoughts or emotions, or otherwise get kudos for being you. You are not writing the final draft of **War & Peace**. Julia Cameron, author of **The Artist's Way**, recommends doing three pages right as you wake up. We are in this wonderful half-asleep, half-awake state, when the mind has very few of its usual protective walls and logical thinking built up around it for the day. This way, you are more able to access your unfiltered thoughts, not the primped for prime-time thoughts. This unfiltered writing can be very helpful in "dumping" a lot of negative mental chatter. If you can't see it, you can't change it.

Consider starting, or re-engaging, your journaling practice and engage a friend for life.

* * *

William (Will) Donnelly *is a nationally recognized, certified yoga teacher and inspirational writer and author. For several years, he partnered with* SpiritualityHealth.com *to offer insightful essays for daily living. Now, his best and most inspirational essays have been re-edited and organized together in his book,* **Practical Yoga's Wisdom for Everyday People**, *which is available at Amazon.com.*

Will has been a pioneer in the field of yoga. He has consistently worked to make yoga accessible. He developed his signature Practical Yoga and co-created the yoga–reality series Guru2Go for fitTV as writer, host, and producer (Discovery Communications, 2004).

Will lives on the magical island of Lana'i in Hawaii, where he is lead yoga instructor at Four Seasons Manale. He has led powerful therapeutic writing classes for many years, and also leads several popular Practical Yoga adventure and healing retreats in Hawaii throughout the year. For more information on his book and streaming yoga DVDs, visit WillsPracticalYoga.com. To pick up a copy of his inspirational book, visit Amazon.com.

Technology Gives You Options—Not Mandates

I'm going to come back to the buffet analogy I used a little earlier this book because it applies here equally as well. Think of the Information Age the same way you think of a buffet as you stand before it. A buffet gives you plenty of options. You get to pick and choose what you want to eat, but you are not required to eat everything.

You also get to pick and choose how much you want to eat, and you get to choose how fast you eat. Lastly, you can eat until you're satisfied, but you're not required to stuff your face and put yourself into a food coma.

A buffet gives you options, but it doesn't give you mandates.

Now, give yourself permission to treat the Information Age the same way! Use technology the way YOU want to use it. Use it when YOU want to use it.

Just like you don't have to stuff yourself with everything you can possibly eat at a buffet, you don't have to overwhelm your senses with every bit of information you can access.

As I mentioned, my colleague Casey Demchak tells me he now only checks his email three times a day. This means he still responds to his emails within 24 hours, which is perfectly fine for his clients.

By only checking his email three times a day he doesn't fall behind and he doesn't miss out on anything, except the mental chaos that used to come with checking his email 20 times a day!

Information overload sucks all the energy out of you, and quite honestly...it can make you nuts. So open your journal, grab your pen, and reflect on how you really feel about technology. What you may find is that a big chunk of the time you currently spend with your smartphone can be better spent journaling, meditating, and reflecting.

Again, information overload can suck all the energy out of you. However, journaling quiets your mind and fuels you with energy and vibrancy. When you journal with a pen in your hand, you're taking a stand and deciding you are going to enjoy a more natural relationship with your mind and your emotions and your heart.

This is important to your wellbeing as a person!

Plus, it's important to know that social-media platforms are designed to get you addicted and give you emotional highs, just like cigarettes, drugs, or booze.

There's a reason why when you grab the scrollbar with your mouse on

Facebook you never get to the bottom of the page. It's because Facebook wants you to keep going! Facebook and other social-media sites program their pages this way because they know we are addictive beings who are highly programmable.

However, we have the ability to pull back from it, and journaling can be an incredible way to get back into an intimacy with yourself rather than being sucked continually into a vortex of electronic crap.

YOU just have to make the effort to take back control! Remember, technology gives you options, not mandates.

Bring Yourself Back to Center

Journaling is one of the most precise ways into the human heart. It's an incredibly powerful tool for you to leverage if you desire to beat back information overload. It's a great way to ground your energy and slow everything down. When you're writing by hand, you can only write so fast. And this is amazingly healthy.

Journaling by hand encourages you to slow down and articulate one idea at a time. It compels you to operate at a more natural pace, be in the moment, and really feel what you're feeling.

When you find you've become too busy to journal, that's when you need to journal the most. Time and time again, journaling will prove its value in terms of its ability to nourish and heal you. It is definitely an antidote to the problem of information overload because it forces you to slow down, breathe, and contemplate.

This is absolute magic for your mind, body, and soul!

Unthread Your Ball of Yarn

If information overload has you anxious, on edge, and ready to scream... grab your pen and pad. Journaling gives you the freedom to unthread the knotted ball of yarn in your gut, and openly communicate anything and everything about your feelings.

It frees you to offload your information-overload madness, instead of expelling it out into the world in unhealthy dysfunctional ways you might regret. If information overload has you feeling like a powder keg, your journal is the perfect place to explode.

When you release your frustration and anxiety in your journal, it becomes a written form of yoga that allows for process and flow. It enables you to clear away that which is clogging your natural radiance.

Write in a slow and thoughtful manner, and you will find it so much more refreshing than the frantic overstimulation you face online. Continue this practice and soon you will anticipate the time you get to spend unwinding and connecting with yourself on a deeper level. And you'll be able to do it at a pace that feels natural and comfortable.

Setting your "Information Age boundaries" through journaling is a peaceful, healthy way to empty out the repressed stress and anger that for many is a byproduct of information overload.

As you step back from the overstimulated e-world, you'll have more time and space to nurture your passions, interests, and gifts you were meant to share with the world.

Remember, your life is about what's going on inside YOU. It's not about what's going on inside your smartphone.

The Lesson in All This

To overcome information overload, you must own and control your mind. You cannot allow your information-technology gadgets to take over your mind and dictate your life to you.

Journaling gives you the perspective you need to train your mind, and the awareness you need to prevent outside stimuli from training it for you.

To keep information overload at bay, you need to train and condition your mind much like you train your pets, which is through repetition and focus. Your journal is the perfect vehicle through which you can do this.

When information overload wins, you lose control of your mind. When this happens, you slip into mental states that can be characterized by words like *stress, frantic, frazzled,* or *angry.*

To prevent this, you have to gain control of your mind and slow things down. Again, journaling is the ideal way to do this. When you slow your mind down as you journal, you gain a certainty that it is your spirit in control of your mind, and not all the crap flying at you a million miles an hour online.

When you use journaling to maintain control over your mind, the gifts you have to share with the world are able to flow forward in a loving way.

Your Journaling Prompt

As I noted earlier, answering questions about your "Information Age habits" is a great journaling prompt for overcoming information overload. The questions I outlined earlier are a good starting point. However, for your prompt, I am going to expand on my initial list.

- How do I feel about my smartphone? Am I addicted to it? Do I feel edgy without it?
- How do I feel about Facebook and my list of friends? How important is this to me?
- Is the time I spend on social media too much? Is it helping me? Is it hurting me?
- Am I addicted to email? Does sorting through my email constantly stress me out?
- Do I hop on social-media platforms even though I know deep down inside I need a break?
- Does social media drain my mental energy and/or make me mad?
- Does how many Likes my last Facebook post received make or break my day?
- Am I venturing into the "e-world" too often to feed some hidden need for attention or approval?
- Can I spend less time with email, texting, and social media, and still lead a full life?
- Can I use new-school tools at a slower pace and still get everything done?

This is a significant list! But if you tap into your heart and are truthful with your answers, you will raise your awareness about how information technology is impacting your life.

This awareness will enable you to spell out new "e-boundaries" in your journal. As you develop and write these boundaries, remember this key point I made earlier:

Technology gives you options, not mandates.

YOU get to choose the influence technology has in your life, and YOU get to retain control of your mind and dictate the pace at which information flows to you.

> *"Journaling is an effective distancing technique. It helps you create an observer perspective where you can step back and see your actions more objectively. This prevents you from drowning in the quicksand of what's going on in your mind with your thoughts and emotions. You instead gain space, perspective, and clarity about what you're actually doing."*
>
> **—Dr. Joe Tatta**, DPT, CNS

Chapter 11

Nurture Your Inner Wisdom

Marie Higgins is a valued member of the Journaling Power revolution, and she has a very interesting story to tell. Marie has an inspiring approach to journaling that she uses to nurture and develop her inner wisdom. I believe strongly that her expressive writing routine can have a profound impact on your life, so I am eager to share it with you in this chapter.

In 2009, Marie did something many only dream of doing. She left the so-called "security" of corporate America, leaving behind a 15-year human-resources-management career so she could take some much-needed time to pursue HER life.

After setting out on her new journey, Marie soon discovered massage therapy and became a nationally certified, state-licensed massage therapist.

Interestingly, Marie began her massage training with no real understanding of the mind-body-spirit connection. But as you know by now, I believe everything happens for reason, and this certainly was the case with Marie.

Through massage, she came to believe in the healing power of touch. At the same time, she felt a partial hardening of the heart (figuratively and spiritually), which led her to seek out a coach who could provide her with a spiritual direction in life.

During this time, Marie learned different spiritual disciplines and ways to pray that helped her develop a more personal relationship with God, or Spirit (*choose the term that works for you*).

It was during this period in 2009 that Marie became active with her journaling. Little did she know at the time that she was joining a revolution!

"God, What Should I Know?"

Over the years, Marie's journaling practice has changed and evolved, but the most constant thing she has put into her practice is to ask a simple question. After she journals what's in her heart or what went on during her day, she simply asks, "God, what should I know?"

When she receives her answer...and she always does...she includes it in her journal. Sometimes the answer comes to her as she sits in silence. Other times she receives the answer by using a tool, such as the Bible or meditation cards.

I think asking this simple question is a fascinating aspect of Marie's journaling practice.

I could go on about it, but it is best explained by Marie herself in a guest blog post she shared with fellow Journaling Power tribe members on CreateWriteNow.com.

Journaling Nurtures Your Inner Wisdom

By Marie Higgins—Author, **Sprouting Spiritual Growth**

What I teach is one of the ways to use journaling to develop your inner spirit wisdom. I recognize that there are many different practices and that individuals can and should modify the steps based on what's best for them. Here is just a starting point with simple steps to follow:

1. Use a journal and write down whatever is on your heart on a regular basis. I do this almost daily now, but when I started years and years ago it was something I did every once in a while, then once or twice a week, and now I hate to miss it. I am a morning person, so I do it first thing or after a few chores.

   It often starts off with what I did the day before or what's coming today, but then I also get into what's bothering me or what's making my heart sing. I might also write my gratitude list in my journal but not always. You decide what time of day is best for you and what you include in your journal.

2. When you think you have written out what's most pressing on your heart, write out the question "God*, what do you want me to know?"
3. Then write down what comes to you. If you feel compelled to use a tool, use a tool. Tools include things like meditation cards (I like the ones with one word on them), a book that you open up randomly and read what's on that page (I often use the Bible or **Psalms for Praying** by Nan Merrill, but non-religious books work too).

If you're not sure what tool to use, let the Spirit* guide you. You might even find your way to my bi-weekly posts that give journaling prompts at cardinaltouch.blogspot.com.

This is the daily practice. It can take as much or as little time as you have. Doing it often provides value because it gives the opportunity to look back over your journey. You can look back over a period of time to see what was happening in your life and what your Higher Power* was telling you, often repeatedly.

Maybe you want to look at the last week, the same week from a year ago, the last whole journal. Whatever time frame is on your heart is right for you. Be a pattern hunter: was the same thing on your heart last year, have you pulled the same meditation card three times in the last month, did you write about the same place or person? Write down what you uncover.

The hard part is making the time to do the work. For me, it has made a significant difference in that I have found an easier way to live, allowing the Great Spirit* to be my guide.

*I use the term God as a universal term. You may decide that Great Spirit, Allah, Higher Power, Sensibility, etc., better suits you today. It is not for me to decide.

* * *

Marie Higgins *is an author and teacher of holistic practices, including meditation and spiritual journaling. She educates individuals on how holistic practices can lead to a simpler life: a way of life that says spirit first (listen to* the heart); second, take care of self (listen to the body), and then give back to the world. Her debut nonfiction piece, **Sprouting Spiritual Growth, a Memoir and a Guide to Spiritual Journaling**, is an inspirational self-help book. It includes ten chapters that provide a guide to get to the truth and beauty of simple everyday living through the tool of spiritual journaling. Her blog site can be found at <u>cardinaltouch.blogspot.com</u>.

Create a Life That Flows

Journaling to nurture your inner wisdom can open your heart and free you from numerous burdens, stress, confusion, and indecision. As you move deeper into this daily form of writing, you'll begin to make a meditative journey inward that becomes more heartfelt with each passing day.

As you connect more and more with yourself, you'll begin to form and create an intimate relationship between you and your God or Spirit. (Again, the *term YOU choose is your own!*) As you connect and speak with Spirit through your journaling, you'll notice a breeziness to your life that you may have not felt before.

Your thoughts will turn from "drama" to gratitude. Your energy will increase as you notice and appreciate the things in life that please you. Over time, you'll begin to notice that your thoughts no longer focus on topics, people, and things that displease you and drain your energy.

Your thoughts will focus on that which pleases and excites you. And you'll pay little interest to things that don't concern or interest you. You'll anticipate the pleasure you're about to feel by engaging in activities and pursuits that arouse and satisfy you. Things that disinterest you or "put a bad taste in your mouth" will be ignored, so that your singular focus is on that which you desire.

The result will be a life that leaves you feeling nourished, quenched, and satisfied. Your life will suddenly move with ease and grace, and you'll feel vibrant and alive like never before.

As you continue to journal to nurture your wisdom…

- Your intuition will intensify and grow stronger
- Things will flow with greater rhythm and meaning

- Ideas and decisions will slip gently into your heart
- Stepping stones revealing your path will appear before you

You'll no longer have to struggle to *make* your best decisions. Instead, you will just FEEL them, and there'll be no doubt in your mind that your decisions are the best ones for YOU.

Space Opens Up for Everything You Want

Continue even deeper into a spiritual journaling practice, and divine timing will begin to play a bigger and more noticeable role in your life. It may even freak you out a little bit. So be prepared!

As you flow in harmony with your Source through journaling, space will open up for everything you want to do. Marie Higgins says that as she continued to nurture her wisdom through expressive writing, divine timing began to play a larger and larger role in her life.

In my conversations with her, Marie would tell me that she would sometimes want to attend classes or social events that had conflicting dates and times, but somehow some way one of the events would be postponed or rescheduled, and space would open in her life for both.

When you connect with your inner wisdom in this deeper fashion, Spirit seems to guide you through your life and lead you down the path on which you're supposed to be.

All you have to know is your ultimate destination, and the stepping stones that will take you there will reveal themselves exactly when they're supposed to.

You'll no longer have to think so hard and wrack your brain. In fact, you'll be able to get out of your head and into your heart. You'll be able to feel your way through life, instead of having to think so damn hard!

Pen-to-paper journaling intended to nurture your inner wisdom will feel like magic to you. Form a daily routine and it will become so meditative and soothing you won't want to miss a day.

Every breath you take will feel fresh and energizing. You'll feel a surge of personal clarity and a certainty of vision. Your mind will no longer race a million miles an hour in twenty-two directions.

Journaling to nurture your wisdom is incredibly grounding, and it's a fantastic way to create an enduring and supportive relationship with YOUR God.

The Lesson in All This

Nearly everyone is intrigued with the thought of getting closer to Spirit and forming a deeper connection with their inner being. People want to believe they have guides or angels that speak to them through their intuition.

Many people spend a lifetime seeking ways to make this connection with their God. They search high and low in their quest to fuel their intuition and make the most of the gifts they were blessed with when they came into this world.

But how do you achieve this connection? What is the secret?

Well, there is no single answer. There are many ways to nurture your wisdom. However, you don't have to travel to the far ends of the Earth to do it; and you don't have to sit for 30 or 40 minutes in a terribly uncomfortable position as you try in vain to blot from your mind the stinging pain in your lower back.

Don't get me wrong, meditation is absolutely magical. But there is another way to connect with Spirit that can become your meditation or become what you do *before or after* you meditate.

The technique you can tap into and leverage to deepen your connection with God is to develop a journaling ritual intended to nurture your inner wisdom. The best part is that all you need to do it is a pen and paper.

As you get into your routine and stick with it, your mind will quiet and that feeling of having a pinball game going on in your head when you wake every morning will disappear.

Instead, you'll awaken to feelings of being present and at one with your God. Messages will flow into your heart. Your focus will be on who or what is in front of you at that moment. What's going in that noisy little world inside your cell phone will become much less of an urgent matter.

You'll feel peaceful and at ease. Your thoughts will be clear and precise. And you may even find that you enjoy listening more than you do talking.

Things that seemed so damn important will slide off into the background until YOU decide it's worth your energy to put your focus on them.

And each time you say, "God, what do you want me to know?"...she will tell you, and you will hear her with absolute clarity and certainty.

Your Journaling Prompt

Your prompt for this chapter is to begin a form of journaling that nourishes and develops your wisdom. You can start by making this a small part of your journaling practice, and then let it naturally develop over time to be a significant part of your journaling practice...or a lesser part...or something in between.

It's up to you. You won't have to think this through; you'll just FEEL it.

So how do you start a journaling practice that nurtures your wisdom? A great way is to begin by finding a place of stillness, ask questions in your journal, and then allow the answers to come to you.

Here are some questions that can prompt a journaling practice that nurtures your wisdom.

- What have I REALLY been doing?
- Is there anything nagging at me?
- Is there something that has really been bothering me?
- Do I have weeds growing in my life? How can I pull them out?
- Are there people who are holding me back in life? Who are they?
- Have I placed self-limitations on myself in life? What are they?
- What are five things I love about myself the most?
- What talents do I feel inside that I'd like to more fully explore?
- What is my purpose? What is my true passion?
- What gift do I have that I really want to share with the world?
- God, what else should I know?

Take your time as you develop this form of journaling. Give yourself time to ease into it.

You may want to start with simple questions and work your way up to more complex questions as you develop your intuition and learn to trust it more as it becomes louder.

And of course, feel free to simply use this list of questions as a guideline. I highly encourage you to build a list of questions that are unique to YOU.

Now, when you ask questions, you may wonder when your answers will come to you. It's different for everyone. They may come to you almost immediately. They may come to you the next morning as you awaken, or when you're meditating, or walking, or gardening.

They key is to ask your questions, relax, and allow them to come to you when they're meant to come to you. Over time, I believe, you will find this to be a very comfortable and gratifying process.

The more you enjoy and have fun with it, the deeper your insights will become.

> *"Journaling brings issues into your consciousness which makes you more aware of them. It brings everything to the surface. Once this happens you become empowered to do something about it. You'll be able to start by asking two questions: Do I want to do something about this issue? And what CAN I do about this issue? When you write down these questions, your intuition will prompt you with the answers you seek."*

—**Jenetta Haim**, Founder of Stressfree Management®;
Lifestyle and Health Management Expert

Chapter 12

Love Yourself More!

I hope you've enjoyed the journaling journey on which I've taken you in *Heal Yourself with Journaling Power.* I hope it has inspired you to tap into the tremendous healing power of journaling that has enabled so many people around the world to transform their lives.

As I wind things down, I want to close with a simple but powerful message. In fact, it may be the most important lesson in this book. And that lesson is this.

The most powerful thing you can do is love yourself. Even if you already do, you can take it to an even higher level through journaling, and I hope you do. I think self-love is the lynchpin of everything I've been writing about, and I think it's something we all can spend more time doing.

If you don't love yourself, who will? If you don't love yourself, how can you expect anyone else to love you as much as you want to be loved?

Now, you don't have to be arrogant or cocky about it, but it is 100% totally fine to be in love with yourself. In fact, I think it's extremely essential to be in love with yourself. I think when you love yourself, you make it much easier for other people to love you too.

Think about it. What have you got to lose by loving yourself? Absolutely nothing.

What have you got to lose by <u>not</u> loving yourself? Absolutely everything.

It's kind of a no-brainer, isn't it? So cut yourself some slack and muster up all the self-love you can.

Your Journaling Prompt

For this final chapter, I want to change things up and jump right into a special journaling prompt. It's simple and straightforward, but it's powerful.

Here's what I'd like you to do. Start a special little section in your current journal. This could be something you add at the beginning of each journal entry, or at the end, or somewhere in the middle. It doesn't matter. Just DO IT!

For your writing prompt, I'd like you to start by just writing "I love myself." And then write it again. And then write it another five times. If you really want to get into it, say it out loud a few times.

Now I know what you may be thinking. You may be thinking, "I've been with you all the way on this journey, Mari...but this is a little silly."

But before you jump to this conclusion, I want to ask you a question: how many times have you written about how much you love yourself?

I'm going to take a wild guess and say not too many times. On the other hand, how many times have you stood in front of your mirror over the years and said things like...

"What the hell's wrong with you?"
"Why'd you do that?"
"How come you're not in better shape?"
"Why don't you have more money?"
"Why don't you try harder?"
"You're worthless."
"You talk too much."

I think we've all said these negative things and more to ourselves in self-anger on occasions. But how many times have you stood in front of your mirror and said:

"I love you! You're awesome!"

If you're not doing it every day, you're not doing it enough. But now you can make up for it by writing it in your journal. All I'm asking you to do is to spend five minutes a day writing down the things you love about yourself.

Just pick one thing each day and shower yourself with some self-love. Maybe it's your eyes, or your determination, or your health, or the "A" you got on a social-studies paper in third grade. Pick anything you want and just DO IT!

I guarantee if you do this, it won't take long before you're going well beyond five minutes, and you will feel fantastic! You deserve this! So get into it and be as joyful as you can about it!

What this exercise does is force you to keep thinking of things you love about yourself. You'd be surprised how many good things can come to you in five minutes if you allow them in.

We've all taken the time to stand in front of the mirror and beat the hell out of ourselves. Now, give yourself five minutes to get the love thing going with yourself in your journal.

Go ahead. After the ass-kicking you've been giving yourself all these years, you deserve five minutes to love on yourself.

After you get in a good groove with this exercise, I encourage you to take it a step further. The way you can do this is to begin writing a list of 100 things you love about yourself.

Your first reaction might be that coming up with 100 things is a bit of a stretch. But you can do it. You may get off to a slow start, but make a commitment to follow through and you'll get there.

In fact, I know that once you get your momentum and energy going, your list will soar well beyond 100, because through this exercise you're going to realize how loveable you really are.

When you complete your list, refer to it often and it will always fill you with confidence and joy. When you allow yourself to feel this way about yourself, it puts you in a tremendous frame of mind for attracting what you really want in all areas of your life.

So I strongly encourage you to do these two things:

1. Spend five minutes each day writing about something you love about yourself.
2. Create a list of 100 things you love about yourself and keep the list handy.

These are two easy things to do. It may not be easy at first, and it may take a few tries to get through five minutes and 100 things. But just DO IT.

Love yourself a lot. It's free and it's simple to do. There are no contracts or memberships to buy, and you can work at it every day in your journal without breaking a sweat.

Getting good at loving yourself can be your own private little thing. No one even has to know you're doing it. You can love yourself while you're writing in your journal every day and no one will suspect a thing.

So go for it. You have nothing to lose and endless amounts of joy to gain.

"When you journal about an aspect of yourself you see as negative, ask yourself, 'Is this thought kind to me?' If it isn't, you need to challenge this and ask if your negative self-comments are going to spur you on to do better, or are they just going to shame you? Because in my experience, self-shame is terrible gasoline for your engine."

—**Dennis Palumbo, M.A., MFT**,
Author and Psychotherapist

* * *

Now, you may be wondering if this is the end of my book-writing journey. Not a chance! I have a lot more to say, so please stay tuned for my next book on this magical life-changing topic for which I have so much passion—the therapeutic and transformative power of journaling.

Lastly, keep writing! Commit to a journaling routine that works for you and stick with it. And remember, there's only one right way to journal—and that's YOUR way.

**Please visit me and the Create Write Now tribe
at <u>www.CreateWriteNow.com</u>.**

Acknowledgements

It takes a village to "build" a book, so I am grateful to everyone who helped bring *Heal Yourself with Journaling Power* to life. First, I'd like to acknowledge all of my fellow Create Write Now tribe members, who fill me with gratitude and inspiration on a daily basis.

It is truly a gift to be able to interact online and in person with such a tremendous gathering of like-minded souls. I am especially grateful to the Create Write Now tribe members who contributed blog posts and allowed me to interview them for this book.

- Jenny Patton
- Antoinette Truglio Martin
- Deb Earleywine
- Ollie Aplin
- Anthony Billoni
- Alison Laverty
- Casey Demchak
- Cheryl Sutherland
- Will Donnelly
- Marie Higgins

In addition, I'd like to thank and acknowledge the expressive-writing experts who provided the insightful pearls of wisdom that are sprinkled throughout *Heal Yourself with Journaling Power.*

- Dr. Joe Tatta, DPT, CNS – www.drjoetatta.com
- Dennis Palumbo, M.A., MFT – www.dennispalumbo.com
- Jenetta Haim, Founder of Stressfree Management® – www.stressfreemanagement.com.au

Lastly, I'd like to thank everyone who has the courage to grab a pen and a pad, open their hearts and minds, and just write! You're all part of a revolution that is making a positive difference in the world.

Please spread the word, and please visit me at www.CreateWriteNow.com.

"We all need to ask ourselves questions about what we're doing and how we're feeling, and what those feelings mean. Journaling is a very good way to do this. And if you're doing it right, it should be more automatic writing and less thinking. Your writing should be flowing freely from your thoughts, moment to moment, impulse to impulse."

—Dennis Palumbo, M.A., MFT,
Author and Psychotherapist

Mari L. McCarthy

Mari L. McCarthy is a personal transformation coach, and the Founder and Chief Inspiration Officer of Create Write Now! She is also author of the international bestselling book *Journaling Power: How to Create the Happy, Healthy Life* You *Want to Live.*

In addition, Mari is the creator of multiple e-Books and Journaling Challenge programs that have had a life-changing impact on countless people around the world.

A former Fortune 100 business consultant, Mari began to experience the debilitating effects of Multiple Sclerosis (MS) 18 years ago, which led to the loss of function and feeling in the right side of her body.

Her doctors, and the prescription drugs they put her on, weren't helping, so Mari began a journey to take control of her own health. After doing some research, she tried a writing therapy known as *Journaling for the Health of It.*

It wasn't easy. Mari had to learn to write with her left hand, but she dedicated herself to daily ACTION and began a journaling practice made popular by Julia Cameron called *Morning Pages*. She never could have anticipated how powerful this process would become.

Through journaling, Mari was able to ditch her prescription drugs and mitigate most of her MS symptoms. Now she teaches people throughout the world how to heal, grow, and transform their lives through the holistic power of expressive writing.

Today, Mari lives in a gorgeous beachfront home in Boston, where she has the freedom, flexibility, and physical ability to indulge in all her passions.

In fact, you'll usually find her writing, singing, reading, walking the beach, meditating, practicing photography, cheering on the Pittsburgh Steelers, and raising roses and consciousness!

Before uncovering her true self through the power of journaling, Mari never dreamed she could become a singer. Well, goodbye to limits! In 2015 she released her **third** album, *Lady With a Song*, and she is currently working on her fourth album, *Well-Written Songs*.

Mari literally created ALL of this through Journaling Power. She now lives life on HER terms, and she is passionately dedicated to helping people around the globe do the same.

CPSIA information can be obtained
at www.ICGtesting.com
Printed in the USA
FSHW022056090619
58891FS